THE EARL OF
DUDLEY'S
RAILWAY

The locomotive that is the most significant 'symbol' of the Earl of Dudley's railway system is *Agenoria* – built by Foster Rastrick in Stourbridge for the opening of the first stretch of railway in 1829. Now to be found at the York Railway Museum. (Ned Williams)

THE EARL OF DUDLEY'S RAILWAY

NED WILLIAMS

The
History
Press

Opposite: Pensnett Railway token.
(Peter Glews Collection)

THE BLACK COUNTRY SOCIETY

The Black Country Society is proud to be associated with **The History Press** of Stroud. In 1994 the society was invited to collaborate in what has proved to be a highly successful publishing partnership, namely the extension of the ***Britain in Old Photographs*** series into the Black Country. In this joint venture the Black Country Society has played an important role in establishing and developing a major contribution to the region's photographic archives by encouraging society members to compile books of photographs on the area or town in which they live.

The first book in the Black Country series was *Wednesbury in Old Photographs* by Ian Bott, launched by Lord Archer of Sandwell in November 1994. Since then over 70 Black Country titles have been published. The total number of photographs contained in these books is in excess of 13,000, suggesting that the whole collection is probably the largest regional photographic survey of its type in any part of the country to date.

The society, which now has over 2,500 members worldwide, organises a yearly programme of activities. There are six venues in the Black Country where evening meetings are held on a monthly basis from September to April. In the summer months, there are fortnightly guided evening walks in the Black Country and its green borderland, and there is also a full programme of excursions further afield by car. Details of all these activities are to be found on the society's website, **www.blackcountrysociety.co.uk**, and in ***The Blackcountryman***, the quarterly magazine that is distributed to all members.

PO Box 71 · Kingswinford · West Midlands DY6 9YN

First published 2014

The History Press
The Mill, Brimscombe Port
Stroud, Gloucestershire, GL5 2QG
www.thehistorypress.co.uk

© Ned Williams, 2014

The right of Ned Williams to be identified as the Author
of this work has been asserted in accordance with the
Copyright, Designs and Patents Act 1988.

British Library Cataloguing in Publication Data.
A catalogue record for this book is available from the British Library.

ISBN 978 0 7524 9308 4

Typesetting and origination by The History Press
Printed in Great Britain

Contents

Many people saw the Earl of Dudley's railway as just an 'internal works system' restricted to the Round Oak Steel Works at Brierley Hill – the kind of image presented in this 1956 picture of the works. The truth, as revealed by this book, is that the railway was a sizable sprawling network stretching in all directions from the hub at Round Oak. While these little shunters were at work twenty-four hours a day in the works, their sister engines ventured far afield. (Jim Houghton)

Acknowledgements

As this book has been a long time in the making, a great many people have helped in many different ways, sometimes providing photographs or first-hand memories of the railway, sometimes assisting in much less obvious ways. Many key figures have died, leaving me wishing that I had asked more questions or made better note of what I was being told. The late Keith Gale was always keen to pass on information about the railway while at the same time making it clear that he preferred to reminisce about blast furnaces and rolling mills. Viv Morgan has always led the way in promoting interest in the Pensnett Railway and has given me valuable assistance. Everyone else I will arrange in alphabetical order, and I apologise to anyone who has been left out.

I would like to thank: Ray Bush, Roger Carpenter, Roger Crombleholme, Arthur Croughton, Elaine Davies, John Dew, Paul Dorney, Peter George, Peter Glews, Les Gregory, Michael Hale, Alan Hallman, Stan Hill, Keith Hodgkins, Jim Houghton, John James, Phil Jones, Vernon Lovatt, Brian Lowe, Robert Millward, Gordon Nutt, Jim Peden, Jack Reynolds, Ray Shill and the Industrial Railway Society, Nick Smith, Roy Simcox, Peter Shoesmith, Tim Shuttleworth, Vic Smallshire, Colin Storey, Val Worwood.

Every author needs someone to support his or her labour, and once again I thank Terri Baker-Mills for persuading me to take the occasional holiday to forget about the mysteries of the Pensnett Railway.

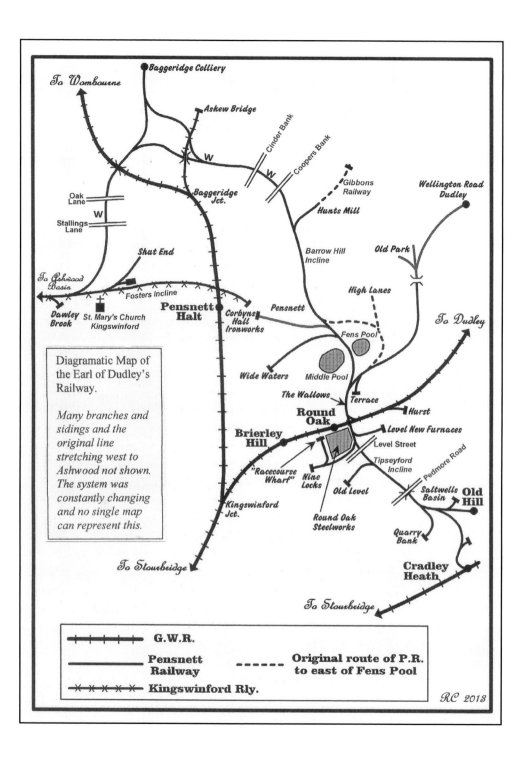

Diagramatic Map of the Earl of Dudley's Railway.

Many branches and sidings and the original line stretching west to Ashwood not shown. The system was constantly changing and no single map can represent this.

Legend:
- G.W.R.
- Pensnett Railway
- Kingswinford Rly.
- Original route of P.R. to east of Fens Pool

RC 2013

Introduction

The Earl of Dudley's railway was an independent industrial railway hidden away in the south-western corner of the Black Country. Although it stretched at one time for about 40 miles, and had a history running from 1829 to 1982, there is very little to be seen of its one-time existence today. Its last steam locomotives were withdrawn in 1963, cut up for scrap metal and sacrificed to the hunger of a steel-making furnace. That all happened fifty years ago and therefore we are approaching the time when such things disappear from living memory. It is true that the railway survived another twenty years in the service of the Round Oak Steel Works in Brierley Hill, and it is true that some of the railway's diesel electric locomotives even survive today, but the general feeling is that the Pensnett Railway, as it was usually known, belongs to a long-vanished world which we can now treat with some degree of nostalgia. Now we can wish that we had taken more notice of such things at the time, and now is the opportunity to put it all on record in the hope we can make sure its story finds a place in posterity.

I arrived in the Black Country in September 1962 and had no idea of what to expect of my new home. By way of introduction, Jack Aldiss, the lecturer in geography at Dudley Training College, gave me and a few others several tours of the Black Country in his battered Bedford Dormobile. On the first trip we went to the top of Sedgley Beacon to see if we could see the Urals on the horizon. On the second trip we headed west to places like Kingswinford and Stourbridge. Returning to Dudley, we paused to gaze at the Delph Locks and then drove through Brierley Hill. Jack could drive while using both hands to point out things of interest on our left and right, and as we came to the end of Brierley Hill, he was using his right hand to persuade us to take in the majesty of the Round Oak Steel Works, and a moment later was gesticulating to the left to draw our attention to the scene at The Wallows. I am sure we slowed down as we gazed at the railway tracks, shed-like buildings, and assortment of steam locomotives. It was a dream-like image that I will never forget.

Of course, I immediately resolved to return to the scene, and possibly I even resolved that I should photograph it. Unfortunately I did not honour this resolution. One reason was that I did not understand how quickly such scenes were going to vanish. The other reason is that I had totally underestimated how many distractions my life in the Black Country would provide.

About eight months later, sometime in 1963, I was still exploring the Black Country on my motorcycle. I decided to leave my motorcycle by a railway overbridge on the Himley Road, and I set out to walk along the railway tracks below. The tracks immediately divided and the rails to the right were very overgrown and seemed to have become the home of a row of semi-derelict railway wagons. The rails to the left led through some trees and down to a complex of sidings and pointwork that totally confused me. I had stumbled across the location at Askew Bridge where the line from Baggeridge Colliery met the former main line of the Pensnett Railway and a spur to the Western Region of British Railways at Baggeridge Junction. I knew nothing of this at the time – to me it was just a bewildering arrangement of tracks, some of which were inhabited by aged and decrepit open wagons. (I found out later that items in the Black Country that looked derelict and abandoned were often really still in use.) I did not make a connection between what I encountered on that day with what I had seen at The Wallows in 1962.

Sometime later I returned to the bridge on the Himley Road (see page 62), and walked up the railway tracks in the other direction. I don't know whether I was expecting to find myself at a colliery, but to my delight I suddenly came across a Hunslet 0-6-0 saddle tank and a row of coal wagons. The colliery was still a short way off. I took one photograph of the locomotive and then spoke to the footplate crew who were surprised to see that I was carrying an 8mm cine camera. They invited me on board and suggested that I film the journey down to Askew Bridge. I shot some film but still failed to ask the questions that would have led to a better understanding of what I had seen.

In 1964 I moved to a flat in Pensnett Road, Holly Hall, in one of the houses that had once been part of Low Town. My landlord, who called himself The Low Town Launderette Company, explained that I could warm the place with a coal fire, and that coal was available 'free' from a local source. All I had to do was arm myself with a bucket and leave the back of the premises by taking a track that had once been the main street of Low Town. Before reaching the shore of Fens Pool, I would encounter a railway track and I was advised to follow that to a point on the far side of the pool where I would find some railway locomotives and wagons that were being scrapped. When I did come to these sidings, I found my neighbours, all armed with buckets, salvaging the coal from the locomotive tenders and the open wagons. I still did not understand where I was in relation to The Wallows, or how I was gradually becoming acquainted with the Pensnett Railway.

From my home in Pensnett Road I could hear the occasional passage of a diesel locomotive running from The Wallows to the Old Park Engineering Works

Coming across semiderelict wagons on very overgrown tracks in the Himley Wood in the 1960s did not help the author put together a coherent picture of the Pensnett Railway. (Viv Morgan)

– the locomotives were fitted with bells that warned everyone of their presence – but not really awakening me to what had passed and what was passing. Like everyone else in the area, I enjoyed the moment when the open-hearth furnaces at Round Oak lit the clouds with a red glow, but I still failed to go round to the steelworks to find out what had happened to its railway.

Several things happened in 1967 to 'awaken me'. Early in 1967 I was working at Dudley's employment exchange and one of my jobs was to go to Baggeridge Colliery to meet miners who were about to face redundancy. My job was to discuss their employment future, but what these meetings did for me was to make me feel that I had shamefully failed to explore the coal-mining history of the Black Country, and that such a history needed better recording. I decided that I should visit pits, and possibly steelworks, whenever possible.

Later in 1967 I found myself working at the Wulfrun College in Wolverhampton. A lecturer who had just left the college returned to tell everyone that he had started a new organisation: the Black Country Society. The inaugurator of this was John Fletcher, and, such were his powers of persuasion, most of us joined his new society straight away. My new job opened many doors into the industrial Black Country world, and the Black Country Society introduced me to other like-minded enthusiasts who all felt the place was worth talking about – its past, present and future.

From that period onwards everything snowballed in every direction. My activities ranged from taking students on trips to collieries and steelworks, to starting a college-based project on the history of the nearest railway line. The latter was the railway to Wombourn, and as I explored the southern end of this line I found myself back in the world once served by the Pensnett Railway. My interest in such matters increased when I had the chance to work for brief spells in local steelworks – first at Bilston and then at Round Oak in about 1970. Meanwhile I was making the acquaintance of local railway enthusiasts like Michael Hale, becoming aware of my ignorance and suddenly realising what I had missed by taking my eyes off the ball for most of the 1960s. I knew that for the next half-century I would have to work hard to understand the Black Country, to comprehend its transport, social and industrial history, and have time to pursue other obsessions. I had completed one book on the Wombourn line, was working with Michael Hale on the history of the railway to Halesowen, and soon generated a list of future projects which at some stage would include looking at the railways of the Earl of Dudley.

Meanwhile, others had already devoted much time and effort to studying the Earl of Dudley's railway. One of these fans of the Pensnett Railway was Thomas Michael Hoskison. Hoskison's father had been appointed manager of the Level New Furnaces in the mid-1920s, having previously worked in colliery management.

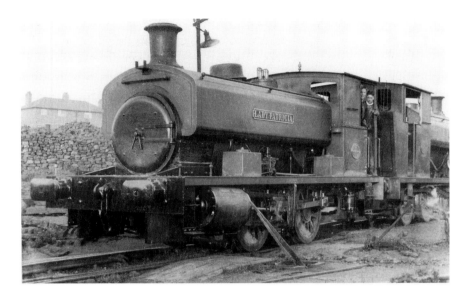

Lady Patricia (Andrew Barclay 1880 of 1925) photographed in 1935. Those alive today who remember steam on the Pensnett Railway prior to its withdrawal in 1963 will recall a railway dominated by Andrew Barclay 0-4-0 and 0-6-0 tanks. (Roger Carpenter Collection)

T.M. Hoskison and Keith Gale collaborated on writing up the history of the Pensnett Railway, the former bringing his intimate first-hand knowledge of the line, and the latter contributing his professional expertise as a writer on technical matters.

They undertook a number of journeys on the Pensnett Railway in 1950 and early 1951, and Michael Hoskison conducted a great deal of painstaking research in the papers of the Priory Estate (i.e. the Earl of Dudley's estate, administered from the Priory Office). By the end of 1951 they had produced a good account of the railway, but for some reason it was not published at that time – they simply left a copy of the text in Brierley Hill Library.

By the 1960s they had decided to publish their text and approached John Horsley Denton of the Cottage Press, in Codsall. Unfortunately, its progress towards publication was extremely slow. Thomas Michael Hoskison died in 1965 while on holiday in Peru. The book finally appeared in 1969, and I went over to John Horsley Denton's home to purchase my copy.

Keith Gale was not happy with the outcome of this project and took advantage of an offer from Goose & Son to produce a slightly updated version in 1975. Even in the new version there was only minimal illustration – an opportunity seemed to be missed. I started visiting Keith Gale in the mid-1980s and was surprised to find that he had a number of photographs of the Pensnett Railway but had always thought of them as 'too recent' to be of any interest. I persuaded Keith that many people would find such pictures interesting and I started using the pictures wherever I could – for example, in 1994 I was able to use some of them in a book about Dudley's railways. Unfortunately, Keith Gale had died in April 1993 and therefore never lived to hear people's appreciation of such pictures.

Meanwhile, I had found other enthusiasts who shared an interest in the Pensnett Railway – particularly Viv Morgan who had already developed considerable knowledge about the line. I was also indebted to Phil Jones who passed on photographs taken by Arthur Croughton and had also been granted access to photographs by Tim Shuttleworth and Ralph Russell. Once there had been a time when it seemed unlikely that a history of the Pensnett Railway could ever be adequately illustrated, but by the 1990s it looked a different proposition.

There were folks at Round Oak who had always recognised the importance and interest of the Pensnett Railway. The works had produced its own staff journal – *The Acorn* – and its pages had often been devoted to the railway. The spring 1957 edition of *The Acorn* gave a good account of the Pensnett Railway, and this proved so popular it was turned into a small booklet. It was the work of Reginald Bashforth, who was editor of *The Acorn*, and he drew heavily on the work of Messrs Hoskison and Gale. In 1974, George Chatham produced his tribute to the railway in the form of a booklet called *Steam at Round Oak*. The book's passage through the production process was assisted by Harold Parsons, editor of *The Blackcountryman*, who was also helping Michael and Hale and myself propel a book on the railway to Halesowen through the same process. We were introduced to George who, at the time, was trying to create something of an archive relating to both the steelworks and the railway. Photographers like Douglas Heath had helped photographically record passing historical moments at the steelworks. There was some optimism about the prospects of recording such material, but this mood faded in the early 1980s when the closure of Round Oak Steel Works became a reality.

My response to the Pensnett Railway has almost been in inverse proportion to the presence of the line itself. In the 1960s, when I could have explored it properly, I completely failed to put together my few brief encounters with the railway. In the 1970s when there were still plenty of people around to talk about the railway, I still accepted that the Gale and Hoskison account of the railway was all that could probably be produced. By the 1980s and '90s it suddenly seemed that the Pensnett Railway had somehow slipped into the past – its remains were rapidly disappearing from the landscape.

In 2012 two events encouraged me to think that it was worth returning to the subject of the Pensnett Railway. Firstly, as a result of producing three books about Brierley Hill for The History Press, I realised that memories of the railway, or of Round Oak Steel Works, still linger on. Secondly, The History Press published

Some parts of the Pensnett Railway were hardly photographed at all. Luckily, Keith Gale took some photographs while travelling over the system in April 1950, and reveals *Lady Morvyth* taking water at the No. 8 pit site near Oak Lane on the important stretch of line which linked the two systems (the Kingswinford Railway and the Pensnett Railway) in 1865 (compare this with the picture on page 67). (Keith Gale)

Paul Collins' book about the Kinver Light Railway. This was a railway, or tramway, that had closed as long ago as 1930, but Paul's fresh look at the subject showed that interest can still be created in such local legends. This made me feel that the story of the Pensnett Railway should be told one more time, and that photographs could play a great part in making it all come to life – even for those who never saw the real thing.

Long may the Pensnett Railway be remembered!

A Note on Names

It will quickly become apparent that the history of this railway system is complicated and that the railway itself was always changing. In the interests of clarity the following names will be consistently applied to the different part of the system:

The Kingswinford Railway: the original line of the Earl of Dudley's railway, opened in 1829, between Shut End and Ashwood Basin.

The Kingswinford Branch: the railway as a branch of the Oxford, Worcester and Wolverhampton Railway, firstly from Kingswood Junction to Bromley Basin (1858) and then on to Askew Bridge and Oak Farm (1860). This became part of the Great Western Railway and subsequently the Western Region of British Railways. The branch was incorporated into the line that ran from Wolverhampton via Wombourn from 1925 until 1965. After this date it almost reverted to its original form, and was often known as the Pensnett Branch.

The Pensnett Railway: the railways built by the Earl of Dudley from the 1840s onwards centred on Round Oak. As from 1865 onwards, these lines were joined to the original Kingswinford Railway and the unified system is always best known as the Pensnett Railway.

The Shut End Railway: the railway built to serve the Shut End Iron Works of John Bradley & Co., eventually taken over by H.S. Pitt & Co. and that company's successors. The line survived to become associated with the Pensnett Trading Estate, although its tracks had been altered many times.

Buildings and rolling stock never carried the legend 'Earl of Dudley's Railway' or 'Pensnett Railway', but buildings included plaques with 'ED' inscribed on them, plus the date and initials of his lordship's agent. Wagons sported the initials 'ED', and, in the final years, 'PR'. (Keith Gale)

1

Historical Outline

1829 And All That

At one time every schoolchild learnt there were two significant dates in English history. One date was 1066, the other was 1829. We learnt that during the latter year the Rainhill Trials were won by Stephenson's *Rocket* and this was followed by the opening of the Liverpool and Manchester Railway. Railways had arrived on the scene to push forward the Industrial Revolution and launch a new era of transport history. For those who wished to delve a little deeper, the story of the Industrial Revolution was more complicated: there were stories of mineral-carrying railways developed earlier in the north-east of England, and occasionally canals were given a mention. There were many such factors in the relationship between industrial progress and transport history.

Today we recognise that industrial and transport history between 1750 and 1850 was very complicated and there were many events and initiatives that jostle for a place in the story, ranging from Enclosure Acts to pumping engines, and to the question of who paid for what. However, if we return to the events of 1829 we still find a convenient point for this story to begin, even if we then have to retrace our steps to try and understand how these events came about.

On Tuesday 2 June 1829, large crowds assembled in the Pensnett area of South Staffordshire to witness a historical event. It was reported in *Aris's Gazette*, a Birmingham-based early newspaper, and thus we know all about it. The account carried the headline: 'Locomotive Engine: Opening of Shut End Railway'. We learn that the spectacle began with a train of four loaded coal wagons making the descent of a rope-worked incline from the Earl of Dudley's colliery near Corbyn's Hall. At the foot of the incline the wagons were attached to a further eight wagons filled with invited guests and *Agenoria* – the 'locomotive engine' – took charge of the train.

Accompanied by a 'band of music' the train then traversed the new railway, carrying coal and passengers to the head of another inclined plane at the other end of the system – way out in the country – where the coal wagons could be lowered to a new canal basin. The train had completed its 3-mile journey at a moderate 7 miles an hour, but *Agenoria* and the crowds then returned to Pensnett for further experiments. This time twelve coal wagons came down the incline and were attached to the open wagons used for conveying passengers. The twenty-wagon train, weighing over 130 tons, then set off on a second trip. It was reckoned that there were 920 passengers onboard, supplemented by up to 300 members of the crowd who decided to hang on the wagons for an unofficial ride. The train travelled at 3½ miles an hour and it was remarkable that there were no accidents.

On the return from the second trip *Agenoria* was allowed a third journey as a 'light engine', although about twenty people managed to cling on to the engine and tender to experience travelling at over 11 miles per hour. This brought the day's work to a close, and the crowds dispersed. Among the guests were the Earl of Bradford and J.H. Foley, the MP for Droitwich, and many industrialists from Birmingham. The proceedings were probably watched over by Messrs Rastrick and Foster, whom we will meet in a moment. However, readers may be surprised that there is no mention of the Earl of Dudley. Technically it was not his 'locomotive engine', but surely it was his railway?

Agenoria and admirers pose for a fine Victorian photograph in about 1870. (Dudley Archives Collection)

What Happened Before 1829?

The eighteenth century was a great time of change. The Industrial Revolution transformed Britain, and areas that had been quiet backwaters suddenly became of great importance and centres of great activity. The more we learn about this process, the more complicated the story looks. The background to the building of the Earl of Dudley's railway reflects this complexity.

South Staffordshire, in an area that was to become known as the Black Country, was an area of potential mineral wealth. Coal, ironstone, limestone and clay were all minerals that lay beneath its surface waiting to be exploited. The questions that had to be resolved were: who owned this mineral wealth? Who would develop the technologies to realise the wealth? Who would capitalise such ventures? And what part would transport play in conveying these minerals and the final products that processing of such minerals might produce?

From just south of the Staffordshire town of Wolverhampton, a ridge, almost 800 feet above sea level, stretched from Sedgley to Rowley. This north-west to south-east line was slightly broken at Dudley where the ridge breaks into separate hills, on one of which stands a castle which was once home to the Lords of Dudley. The very geomorphological forces that created this ridge also pushed the underlying strata of coal close to the surface on either side of the ridge. Some of this coal was to be found in a spectacular 10-yard seam, often close to the surface.

The area to the north and east of this ridge enjoyed easier access to this mineral wealth. It was flatter and was more easily connected to the outside world. The area to the south and west of the ridge posed more problems. The two halves of the Black Country therefore experienced slightly different patterns of development, and the Earl of Dudley's railway is part of the story of the south-west side of the Black Country's progress.

The most important landowner in Dudley and the area to the south and west of the town was the Ward family. A key player in our story is John, 2nd Viscount of Dudley and Ward, who succeeded to the title and ownership of the Dudley estates in 1774. He immediately set about improving communications and developing industry, and made sure his interests were well served by the passing of the Enclosure Acts.

As a result of the Enclosure Acts passed towards the end of the eighteenth century, the Ward family was able to consolidate its grip on the industrial development of the area. The Ashwood Hay and Wall Heath Enclosure Act of 1776 dealt with an area of 14,000 acres which included what would become the western terminus of the Earl of Dudley's railway, although this act does not mention industrial matters or use the word 'railway'. Two further acts, passed in 1784, are quite different in this respect. The Dudley Enclosure Act and the

Kingswinford Enclosure Act both mention that the Lord of the Manor has the right to 'make use of all convenient ways, roads, and railways required in connection with collieries, mines and other mineral workings'.

This eighteenth-century reference to 'railways' referred to simple wagonways on which horse-drawn wagons would provide transport. Two other contributors to transport history were also making an impact at the same time: the turnpike road and the canal. The south-western half of the Black Country was going to be a rich area of turnpike development, but canal building was going to be more of a problem. This was probably why no mention of canals is made in the Enclosure Acts mentioned above. However, the Rowley Regis Enclosure Act of 1799 does mention canals, as well as furnaces and ironworks.

Almost as soon as canals were demonstrated as viable propositions, their development was seen on a grand, national scale as well as a solution to very local transport problems. Little wonder, therefore, that the Staffordshire and Worcestershire Canal is proposed as a link from the Severn to the Trent, and selects a route that seems to bypass the industrialisation of the south-west section of the Black Country. The canal opened in 1772. Ashwood, out in the Smestow Valley, is as close as this canal comes to the area we are looking at.

In 1792, the Dudley Canal Tunnel was opened and provided access from the area to the south and west of the ridge to the Birmingham–Wolverhampton system of canals on the other side of the ridge. The Dudley Canal continued down to Brierley Hill and terminated at the foot of the Delph Locks. At this point it joined the Stourbridge Canal, which had approached the Delph from Wordsley. (From the latter point, the Stourbridge Canal had a branch into Stourbridge itself.) Beyond Wordsley, the Stourbridge Canal made its way to Stourton where it was able to join the Staffordshire and Worcestershire Canal. Both the Dudley Canal and the Stourbridge Canal opened in 1779 and were supported by the Earl of Dudley, proprietor of nearby collieries.

The Stourbridge Canal brought its system very close to the area described by this book. The company's reservoirs were constructed on Pensnett Chase and became known as Fens Pool, Middle Pool and Grove Pool. The water from these pools was taken via a branch of the system to the main line of the Stourbridge Canal at a place called The Leys, near Brockmoor. Not far from The Leys it was proposed, during the 1820s, to build another stretch of canal up to Shut End – right in the heart of our area of interest. However, nothing immediately came of the proposal and this lack of activity seems to have prompted the Earl of Dudley's interest, as the 1820s progressed, in linking the Shut End area with the Staffordshire and Worcestershire Canal via a railway.

In conclusion, as far as the story told so far is concerned, the early canal system did not immediately serve the local needs of the Earl of Dudley. The second wave of canal development was closer to his doorstep but still failed to bring the canal system into the heart of the area around Pensnett. By the 1820s this may have made the prospect of building a railway more alluring, but by the 1830s the prospects of building a canal to Shut End were reinvigorated, resulting in the building of the Stourbridge Extension Canal.

Enter Key Players

The Earls of Dudley managed the exploitation of the mineral wealth of their estates, and the parallel industrialisation, via the work of an agent or steward. At the beginning of the nineteenth century the work was carried out by John Keeling, but he died in 1823 and was replaced by a mining engineer named Francis Dowling. Three years later Dowling's job title became a little more focussed when he became his lordship's mineral agent. It is John Dowling who must have played a key part in working out that a railway might assist in transporting coal from the pits to a suitable point on the new canal network. It is therefore John Dowling's signature that appears on an agreement made on 17 January 1827 with a gentleman named James Foster.

James Foster (1786–1853) became sole proprietor of John Bradley & Co., iron and coal masters of Stourbridge, in 1816 upon the death of his partner and stepbrother, John Bradley. The company had been established by John Bradley, and some partners, and had begun its activities in 1800. Within a couple of years the company had become specialists in the manufacture and sale of iron, based in a works not far from the end of the Stourbridge Canal. The 1827 agreement to build a railway involved crossing land owned by the Earl of Dudley and sometimes crossing property leased to Foster. Where the proposed line crossed the property of a third party, such as John Foley, then further agreements were necessary. James Foster was anticipating the development of collieries and an ironworks at Shut End, while the Earl of Dudley had pits in the surrounding area. John Foster also played a part in supplying the railway with its sole locomotive.

Construction

After the signing of the 1827 agreement, construction of the railway commenced and building a locomotive to work the line also began. Although nothing is known about who built the railway, a great deal is known about building its locomotive. The railway was to start at a new canal basin built at Ashwood on the Staffordshire and Worcestershire Canal. Immediately after leaving the basin, the line would ascend an incline 500 yards long at a gradient of 1 in 28. At the top of the incline, the railway's main line would then stretch eastwards for a distance of nearly 2 miles. This stretch was regarded as level but did slightly climb as it made its way through Wall Heath, past the Dawley Brook area of Kingswinford, and on towards Shut End. At Shut End the railway traversed another incline – 1,000 yards in length at a gradient of 1 in 29. This would have to be chain-worked from an engine house at the upper end. From the top of the incline the line curved to the south and crossed the Dudley–Kingswinford road. The line terminated at a colliery owned by the Earl of Dudley close to Corbyn's Hall. The landscape has so changed at this end of the line it is difficult to imagine the site of the eastern terminus.

The railway was built to the 'standard gauge' (4ft 8½in) and used 15–18ft lengths of fish-bellied rail laid in chairs supported on stone blocks spaced at 5ft 6in intervals. The inclines had to be carefully engineered, and civil engineering work included building embankments and two bridges over existing roads. At other points there were level crossings, and there was at least one point where a small colliery tram road crossed over the new railway.

As well as building the railway, a new basin had to be built on the Staffordshire and Worcestershire Canal at Ashwood. It was a lengthy basin (sometimes said to be 600 yards long, at other times said to be 750 yards long) which is perhaps an indicator as to the amount of traffic that was anticipated. It exploited the existence of a natural valley but this set the basin at rather an oblique angle to the

Ashwood Basin in about 1950, seen from the road bridge crossing the basin. (Jack Reynolds Collection)

main canal. This was fine for southbound boats but boats heading north had to back out of the basin to do so. Sidings and loading devices were placed alongside both banks of the basin, and the basin itself was crossed by an impressive eleven-arched viaduct carrying a local road. Limekilns and other buildings were also built at the basin, as well as cottage accommodation for some of the Earl of Dudley's staff. Although the basin survives today as a marina, there is little evidence of its original use. It was completed in time for the opening of the railway in June 1829.

This stretch of railway was known by different names, and to distinguish it from other lines that become part of the story, it will be known in this book as the Kingswinford Railway.

Agenoria

Today it is possible to visit the National Railway Museum at York and see *Agenoria* in all her glory (but minus her tender). She was built by Foster Rastrick & Co. of Stourbridge alongside three similar locomotives, which were going to be exported to America. John Urpath Rastrick (1780–1856) joined James Foster at the Stourbridge Works in 1819 and played a part in the design of *Agenoria*. John Urpath Rastrick came from Morpeth where he learnt his trade as an engineer by first being apprenticed in his father's engineering works. He later moved south, and at one stage found himself working with Richard Trevithick in building a high-pressure boiler at Hazeldine's works in Bridgnorth. Rastrick's partnership with Foster lasted until 1831, and they made their fortune by building blast furnace equipment rather than further railway engines. It is interesting to note that a few months after *Agenoria* showed her paces on the Kingswinford Railway in 1829, Rastrick was invited to become a judge at the Rainhill Trials.

Agenoria was a four-coupled locomotive with two vertical cylinders mounted at the rear end of the boiler. The piston rods drove the wheels via a system of connecting rods and beams mounted above the boiler. Water was carried in a primitive tender, and comfort for the crew on the footplate was nil. Most people comment on the height of the locomotive's chimney, but one of its most innovative design features was that the motion of the wheels activated a self-lubrication of the bearings. The 1829 report in *Aris's Gazette* commented on the locomotive's quietness and its moderate emission of smoke and steam.

1829 onwards

After the excitement of the railway's opening at the beginning of June 1829, it seems to have settled down and quietly and efficiently carried out its tasks.

The system remained relatively unaltered, although colliery sidings were probably added and withdrawn as pits came into and went out of use. The major addition to the landscape in which the railway operated came in the form of the Shut End Iron Works.

The Shut End Iron Works was developed by James Foster of John Bradley & Co., and was designed to put new blast furnaces close to the pits that would supply the coal and a limited amount of local ironstone. The first phase of the works was built between 1829 and 1831, and a siding was laid from a junction just north of Kingswinford parish church into the ironworks. The junction was close to the Kingswinford Railway's engine shed, which in turn was close to the start of the incline at the eastern end of the railway. This area therefore became the operating hub of the system. Within a few years the railway was carrying considerable traffic from the Earl of Dudley's collieries plus traffic in and out of the Shut End Iron Works. *Agenoria*'s efforts were probably supplemented by some horse-drawn traffic as she remained the sole locomotive on the system.

As these were the early days of railway operation, there was still a lot to find out about such an undertaking. One eventual problem was the question of maintaining the track.

In 1836, seven years after the railway had opened, Richard Smith became the Earl of Dudley's mineral agent. By 1840, he seems to have realised that track maintenance might be a problem. There was an attempt to find a contractor who could undertake such work and the task was given to one Edward Barnsley of Wolverhampton on payment of £150 per year. He lasted three and half years in the job before falling out with Richard Smith. After 1844, the railway may have employed its own plate-laying and track maintenance staff. By this time, railway construction was being considered in other parts of the Earl of Dudley's empire.

The other thing that happened in the 1830s was the authorisation and construction of the Stourbridge Extension Canal, which has been briefly mentioned earlier. The idea had been abandoned by the Stourbridge Canal Company, but in June 1837 a new Act authorised construction of the Stourbridge Extension Canal from the Stourbridge Canal at a point near The Leys, up through Bromley, out through Shut End, and to a terminus near Oak Farm. At the junction the new canal would include a basin (basically a wider stretch of canal) which would be known as Bromley Basin. The Extension Canal would also add two branches – a short branch near Bromley and a longer one to Standhills. Within its short course the Extension Canal was going to provide access to the numerous pits, ironworks and brickworks which were 'mushrooming' in the area, even if further basins would have to be provided. The Stourbridge Extension Canal opened in 1840, passing under the incline at the eastern end of the Kingswinford Railway.

The Stourbridge Extension Canal had at one time entertained ambitious plans to head northwards via the Cotwall End Valley and even burrow under the ridge to reach the Birmingham Canal near Bloomfield. There was great opposition to such plans at the time but today's readers might wonder why on earth it was worth terminating the canal at Oak Farm. The answer lies with the brief life and times of the Oak Farm Iron Works, owned by Stephen Glynne. (He and James Foster were major shareholders in the Extension Canal.) The Oak Farm Iron Works began to develop in the mid-1830s on quite a large scale but by the end of the 1840s was facing bankruptcy. Glynne's brother-in-law, Gladstone, devoted much of his energies to sorting out its debts when not pursuing his political career. The works had closed by the late 1860s. The area around the works was developing as the Earl of Dudley's Himley Coalfield, at first cut off from the Earl's other activities.

A Further Phase of Railway Planning and Building

In the 1840s, the Earl's mining and industrial activities had become more dispersed. Pits were numbered in series in separate areas of the coalfield. For example, the Himley pits were to be found between Gornal Wood and Pensnett, north of Barrow Hill. The Saltwells pits were to be found south of Brierley Hill, and the Old Park series of pits were to be found closer to Dudley in the area now covered by the Russells Hall Estate. Transport between these areas, and linking pits to canals or works, had to be improved. In 1842, the trustees of the late Earl of Dudley's estate commissioned a consultant, F.P. Mackelcan, to look into further railway development.

The Earl of Dudley, who had been around at the time of the opening of the Kingswinford Railway, had died in 1833 unmarried and without an heir. His cousin became Baron Ward, and the Earldom was declared extinct. By the 1840s a William Ward held the estate – but just to confuse present readers he was made an earl in 1860 thus restoring the title. When we use the term, 'the Earl of Dudley's railway' people have the right to ask which 'earl' we are talking about, but the truth is that it was the estate's mineral agent who provided the continuity and the single strand of railway development. Richard Smith remained in this role until 1864 and then the post was given to his son.

It was therefore Richard Smith, in his role as mineral agent, who had to respond to Mackelcan's suggestions and begin the process that led to the building of what became the Pensnett Railway. In 1843, Mackelcan came up with four suggested lines, three of which were built more or less as he suggested. The suggestion that was dropped was one that would have linked the new lines with the existing Kingswinford Railway by continuing the route taken by Foster's Incline eastwards to the Old Park – meeting the new lines at a point which

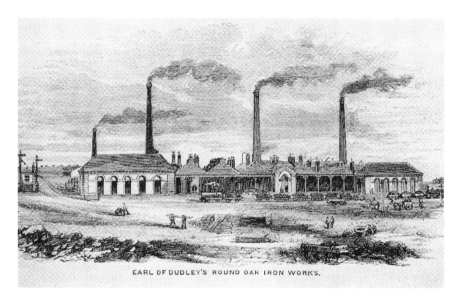

EARL OF DUDLEY'S ROUND OAK IRON WORKS.

The Round Oak Iron Works became the centre of the second phase of railway building to serve the interests of the Earl of Dudley, although at first detached from the railway from Shut End to Ashwood. (Keith Gale Collection)

would have been about halfway down the proposed Barrow Incline. Interestingly, the idea was rejected partly because the incline at Shut End was already adversely affected by subsidence.

The new railways were to include a line from the Himley Coalfield to The Wallows. This would have climbed an incline up the side of Barrow Hill, pass under the Dudley–Kingswinford road, and make for The Wallows by following the eastern shore of Fens Pool. (Not the embankment between the pools with which we are more familiar.) A second line would run between the Level New Furnaces and the top of the Nine Locks on the southern side of the Dudley–Round Oak–Brierley Hill road. A third line would have to connect the other two lines. The first of these three lines became the main line of the Pensnett Railway and involved some significant civil engineering: cuttings and embankments and two stationary engine-worked inclines: one at Barrow Hill and the other just before reaching The Wallows. (Modifications to the railway soon made the latter redundant.)

A contractor named William Hughes began constructing these lines in the mid-1840s.

At this point the story takes an interesting twist because the Oxford, Worcester and Wolverhampton Railway was authorised in 1845 to pass through the same area on its way from Brierley Hill to Dudley. When this section of the OWWR opened in 1852, the Pensnett Railway was already in use. This feeling that the Pensnett Railway got there first is immortalised in the proceedings of the parliamentary

Brandon (Manning Wardle 6 of 1859) seen at Shut End on the Kingswinford Railway. (Keith Gale Collection)

committee that looked into the OWWR's bill. Isambard Kingdom Brunel, as the OWWR's engineer, had to appear before this committee and was asked questions about how his railway was going to cross the Earl of Dudley's railway. The proposal was that the lines crossed 'on the level' but the OWWR appeared to be planning a line at a lower level than the Earl's line. Brunel uttered the famous line: 'If Lord Ward will not alter his railway an inch, we must come to his level.'

Another implication of the OWWR's arrival on the scene was that the company proposed building a branch from just north of Brettell Lane up to Oak Farm – running parallel with the Stourbridge Extension Canal, which the railway company had already acquired. Its significance was that this would eventually provide another link with the Pensnett Railway.

The Pensnett Railway Becomes Established

As William Hughes completed his work the railway was brought into use, although it is not known what locomotives were used until the mid-1850s. By the time the Pensnett Railway's trains and the OWWR's trains were passing over each other's rails on the crossing near Round Oak, from 16 November 1852 onwards, other changes were afoot. At the end of 1851, the sinking had commenced of the first pit in the Saltwells area.

The Saltwells area was the southernmost section of the old Pensnett Chase and consisted of the wooded valleys of the Black Brook and the Mousesweet Brook. These brooks drained water from the Rowley Hills, passed either side of Netherton and met just south of Mushroom Green to reach a confluence with the Stour at Cradley Forge, near Quarry Bank. To reach the area, a new railway had to descend the bank at the back of the ridge on which Round Oak and Brierley Hill stood – thus creating yet another stationary engine-worked incline. Called the Tipsyford Incline, it started just beyond the junction with the rest of the system by Level Street and descended to a point where it could level out and pass beneath the Dudley–Worcester turnpike road and reach the Saltwells pits. This pushed the Pensnett Railway eastwards and southwards into new territory towards Netherton, Old Hill and Cradley Heath.

The mid-1850s also witnessed the consolidation of the Earl of Dudley's iron-making business with the building of an extensive modern ironworks at Round Oak – eventually to become the centre of the private railway system. Although the Dudley Estate had a history of producing pig iron, this had usually been sold on to those who would turn it into wrought iron or finished products. The new works at Round Oak was built to enable the Earl's business to complete these other processes. The furnaces at Round Oak Iron Works commenced production on 28 August 1857.

Once the Round Oak Iron Works was up and running, the Pensnett Railway took on a more complicated identity – or rather a 'split personality'. The outer reaches of the railway still carried coal from pits to canal wharves, or from pits to furnaces, but the other half of the railway's work was that of being an internal works' system. This division in the railway's work lasted over 100 years.

One consequence of the greater work for the railway was that Richard Smith needed to look into the provision of locomotive supply. He sent his son, Frederick Smith, to the Railway Foundry in Leeds. The latter was trading as E.B. Wilson at the time, but was later better known as the Manning Wardle company. The first locomotive from E.B. Wilson was ordered on Frederick Smith's recommendation, and *Alma* was delivered in May 1856. Two similar engines, *Brandon* and *Himley*, followed in 1859 and were the fifth and sixth locomotives made under the Manning Wardle 'label'. *Alma* would have had her work cut out to undertake all was demanded on the Pensnett Railway and the works' system, which reinforces the view that the Pensnett Railway must have had some locomotives available as soon as the lines recommended by Mackelcan came into use.

Another development of the late 1850s also eventually impinged on the story of the Earl of Dudley's railway. The Oxford, Worcester and Wolverhampton Railway opened a goods-only branch from Kingswinford Junction, just north of Brettell Lane, to Bromley Basin on the Stourbridge Extension Canal, on 14 November 1858. Goods to and from the enterprises between Bromley Basin and Shut End could begin or end their journey by canal for the time being. Before pushing northwards, there seemed to be some further debate about where the branch should terminate. By 1860, when the completed branch came into use, it managed to serve two termini, one at Oak Farm, and the other at Askew Bridge, close to the Dudley–Himley turnpike road. The latter indicated the company's intention of serving pits in the Earl of Dudley's Himley Coalfield, and later provided a location in which the Earl of Dudley's railway (the Pensnett Railway) could meet the main-line company. The main-line company itself ceased to be the OWWR in 1860 when it became part of the West Midland Railway, and in 1863 the WMR was absorbed into the Great Western Railway.

The branch to Bromley Basin and on to Oak Farm or Askew Bridge was always known to the main-line companies as the Kingswinford Branch, which seems confusing to the modern reader. It also has to be clearly distinguished from the Kingswinford Railway, which was the Earl's 1829 line from Shut End to Ashwood Basin.

Alma built by E.B. Wilson in 1855 and delivered to the Pensnett Railway in 1856. The similarity of the Wilson and Manning Wardle locomotives was a result of the latter partnership having purchased all Wilson's drawings when the railway foundry ceased trading in 1858. Driver Charles Mace is on the footplate, accompanied by his two sons. (Viv Morgan Collection)

The 1860s and the Creation of a Unified System

In 1864, Frederick Smith followed in his father's footsteps by becoming the Earl of Dudley's mineral agent. By this time, the original Kingswinford Railway was in need of some attention and Frederick Smith had to negotiate with William Orme Foster, who had succeeded his uncle, James Foster, at the helm of John Bradley & Co. Between them they refurbished the Kingswinford Railway and did away with the incline on the approach to Ashwood Basin. The other incline, at Shut End, was already out of use.

The next step was to create a link between the old Kingswinford Railway and the newer Pensnett Railway which had reached some of the Himley pits by descending the Barrow Hill Incline. From Himley No. 3 pit it was only about ¾ mile to a point where it could join the KR just south of Stallings Lane, slightly west of the old engine shed and junction with the line into Shut End Iron Works. It seems that the link between the two lines came into use in 1865.

The 'link' at Himley was not the only addition to the railway being made at this time. The so-called 'upper line' of Mackelcan's proposals ran from Nine Locks in Mill Street, Brierley Hill, through to High Lanes. This was now extended beyond Low Town, under the Dudley–Kingswinford road at the current location of a busy road island by the Russells Hall Hospital, and out into the Old Park. By keeping

Countess was another Manning Wardle of 1859 in the 'Wilson' style and was probably assembled at the Castle Mill Works. Charles Mace is thought to be on the footplate. (Dudley Archives Collection)

to ground close to the main road it was able to extend the line towards Dudley to a new landsale wharf established in Wellington Road. The latter opened on 1 November 1865.

By the end of 1867 the 'unified system' was simply known as the Pensnett Railway.

The 1870s – Links to the Outside World

Sidings and new connections were always being added and subtracted to and from the Pensnett Railway in a rather bewildering manner. In the autumn of 1870, a branch from the Ashwood Basin line was opened to serve the new gasworks at Dawley Brook, just north of Kingswinford. On the other side of Kingswinford, a line was laid to the wharf by the Planet Brickworks by the main Dudley–Kingswinford road.

Of much greater significance were the connections made with the main-line railway system. One such connection was made with the GWR Stourbridge Extension line at Cradley Heath. Only Forge Lane separated a landsale wharf served by the Pensnett Railway from sidings in the GWR's goods yard. In 1874, a line was laid across Forge Lane to make the link. This enabled coal mined in the Saltwells area to leave the Pensnett Railway at this point.

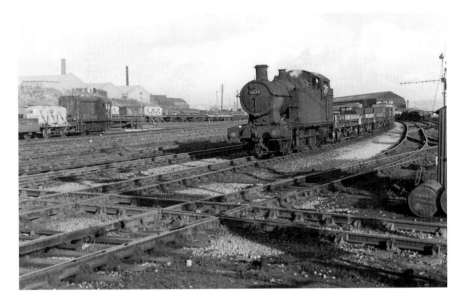

A GWR 54xx class 0-6-2T approaches the famous crossing in about 1960. Note the number of tracks the Pensnett Railway had to cross once sidings were provided on either side of the GWR's running lines. The last traces of the crossing disappeared at the end of 1983. (Viv Morgan)

Another major link with the outside world was created at the Askew Bridge end of the system. The GWR Kingswinford Branch had its Himley terminus just short of the Dudley–Himley road, having passed over the 1865 line that linked the two parts of the Earl's system. In 1875, a short link was put in that joined the two lines, although reversal was necessary at Askew Bridge to reach what later became known as Baggeridge Junction. All this became of greater significance in the twentieth century with the opening of Baggeridge Colliery.

The Pensnett Railway also had to interact with the outside world in the form of the GWR when it came to dealing with the Earl of Dudley's Castle Mill Works. The works began life about the mid-1840s and gradually became the engineering centre of the Earl's empire, capable of building and maintaining 'plant' for the Earl's pits and ironworks. The OWWR reached Dudley in 1852 and became the GWR just over ten years later. At some stage a line was laid from the GWR goods yard to the Castle Mill Works, and thereafter the works could undertake heavy repair and even rebuilding work on the Pensnett Railway's locomotives. Locomotives had to travel between Round Oak and Dudley on GWR tracks, generally under the supervision of an inspector, and were sometimes hauled 'dead' by GWR locomotives. Castle Mill Works closed in the late 1920s and the track from there to Dudley GWR goods yard was lifted.

Changing Times: 1880s and 1890s

During the 1880s quite a few of the original agreements and leases, particularly between the Earl of Dudley and James Foster, had to be re-examined. The decline of the Shut End Iron Works led William Foster, and his local manager, to have less interest in the fate of the railway to Ashwood Basin and the Pensnett Railway took over complete responsibility for the line and the basin. John Bradley & Co. continued to work local traffic within the Shut End area and when necessary handed traffic over to the Pensnett Railway.

The Pensnett Railway remained an operator of just less than 40 miles of railway and continued to be very busy. It was now managed by Joshua Mantle, and a little is said separately about the Mantle family and their involvement with the Pensnett Railway later in this book. In 1892, a short branch, about ½ mile long, was built to provide rail access to Joseph Penn's Providence Iron Works on the outskirts of Old Hill. This became famous after a spectacular boiler explosion in 1906.

Meanwhile, an important, but often overlooked, modification to the Pensnett Railway system had been made at the beginning of the 1880s. Instead of the main line heading north from The Wallows and circumnavigating Fens Pool on its eastern shore, a new, more direct route was taken between Fens Pool and Middle Pool. Putting in this line entailed building the embankment that now separates the two pools. Probably a modest embankment existed there beforehand but it must have been enhanced for its new role. The work was finished by 1883, but the large-scale ordnance survey map of that year must have been surveyed earlier and that is why the map shows the railway still running round the eastern end of Fens Pool. Some of the old line was retained as it provided access to the Old Park Brickworks, which once occupied ground south of the Dudley–Kingswinford road opposite the present Russells Hall Hospital. A short stretch of the old line also survived as part of what became a branch to the Old Park and Dudley.

It is also difficult to imagine that the old route round the eastern shore of Fens Pool also provided access to a branch that took the railway down to The Wide Waters – a basin at the end of the canal feeder between the northernmost limits of the Stourbridge Canal and Grove Pool. The Wide Waters can still be explored by joining the canal at the bridge on Pensnett Road near The Dell playing fields, but it is yet another area that has undergone great changes.

By the 1890s many of the small pits in Himley, Saltwells and Wallows districts were becoming worked out. Areas such as the Old Park and around Netherton were already abandoned, derelict wastelands. Equally significant was the decline in the iron-making industry, and local iron ore had been exhausted for some time. Steel was a serious challenge to wrought iron, and many local ironworks were unable to convert to steel production. A steel-making plant was installed at Round Oak in 1894, and wrought iron production was phased out, although pig iron continued to be made at the Level New Furnaces.

Right at the end of the nineteenth century, the Pensnett Railway acquired some new traffic as a result of Messrs Gibbons building a railway from their brickworks at Dibdale to the Pensnett Railway at the foot of the Barrow Hill Incline, where there was yet another brickworks established near Hunts Mill. The Gibbons Railway had its own locomotives which handed traffic over to the Pensnett Railway for conveyance to Askew Bridge or Round Oak.

Into the Twentieth Century

In the early years of the twentieth century several elderly Pensnett Railway engines were substantially rebuilt at the Castle Mill Works, while much attention was being given to the quest for coal beyond the boundary faults of the South Staffordshire Coalfield. If new deep sources of coal could be accessed, the Pensnett Railway could look forward to a future for its lines outside Round Oak. Efforts centred around the sinking of a shaft at Baggeridge, after geological surveys in the Cotwall End Valley led nowhere. The first shaft was sunk at Baggeridge in 1898 but serious work on creating the pit did not begin until the mid-1900s.

A narrow gauge railway was built from Himley No. 5 pit, served by the standard gauge Pensnett Railway, up through the woods to the site of the proposed colliery. This was sufficient to deal with the small amount of traffic generated while the colliery shaft was sunk. In anticipation of heavy traffic, the Pensnett Railway planned a standard gauge line from Askew Bridge up to the new pit and it was agreed that the GWR would take responsibility for its construction as coal would also traverse the line to reach the GWR at Baggeridge Junction.

In August 1906, the GWR signed a contract with Henry Lovatt of Wolverhampton to build the railway – about 1¾ miles long to Baggeridge Colliery. It was built to GWR standards but was always to be worked by the Pensnett Railway. The colliery did not start production until 1912.

Meanwhile, in 1910 the Pensnett Railway was formally introduced to interested members of the public for the first time. This took the form of a two-part article in a monthly magazine called *The Locomotive*. It was written by T.R. Perkins, an enthusiast determined to travel over every mile of railway in Britain. He was shown round the system by one of the Mantle family and traversed most, but not all, of the line, and took photographs. He travelled on the locomotive *Queen*, which had just been rebuilt at the Castle Mill Works. As he spent quite a lot of time looking at all there was to see at The Wallows, he did not have time to travel on the branch to Wellington Road, Dudley. He did, however, descend the Tipsyford Incline and reached the Saltwells area. As an enthusiast of that time, he was more interested in locomotives than the geography of the area through which the line travelled, but he still provides the reader with a fascinating glimpse of the Pensnett Railway at work.

Four years later the First World War began and the Pensnett Railway struggled on with increased traffic but declining maintenance. By the end of the war the railway had just the required number of working engines to meet its commitments – there was no 'slack' in the system to cope with repairs and overhauls. Two new Peckett locomotives arrived in 1921 and were put to work on the Barrow Hill Incline. It was hoped that more powerful locomotives would result in the incline no longer needing to be cable-worked. By the mid-1920s, locomotives of sufficient power were making their own way up the incline.

During the mid-1920s the role of the Castle Mill Works declined and the Pensnett Railway took greater responsibility for maintaining its locomotives and rolling stock at the expanding facilities at The Wallows, which had been the operating and administrative hub of the line for many years. Then came what many considered to be the railway's finest hour – its annual operation of passenger trains to take Round Oak employees to the Earl's fetes in the grounds of Himley Hall. The annual August holiday passenger trains to Himley are described in a separate chapter.

Lady Rosemary (Peckett 1517 of 1921) represented the quest for more powerful locomotives capable of propelling trains up the Barrow Hill Incline unassisted. Such engines were later replaced by powerful Andrew Barclay 0-6-0STs. *Lady Rosemary* was scrapped after the Second World War, but by that time the name was being carried by one of the Andrew Barclay 0-4-0 STs. (Peter Glews Collection)

End of an Era

By the outbreak of the Second World War the Pensnett Railway had passed its zenith. The lines in the Saltwells area had particularly declined in the 1930s, despite the existence of 'The Earl's Muck Works' close to where the railway crossed Saltwells Road. Slag from the steelworks was brought down the Tipsyford Incline and taken along to these works where it was processed and bagged. The pits of the Himley Coalfield were also largely worked out, although Baggeridge Colliery continued to be an important user of the railway. The war saw a great deal of activity at the Round Oak Steel Works and on the Pensnett Railway, and even some pits – like Himley No. 4 – were temporarily reopened. The railway did acquire some new locomotives from Andrew Barclay during the war to help maintain its services.

As life returned to normal after the war, the contraction of the Pensnett Railway, which had begun before the war, gained momentum. The line to Cradley Heath was down to one or two trains a day and these were withdrawn as the 1950s began – and the rails were lifted by 1952. Only the top part of the Tipsyford Incline was retained to provide access to the finishing mills on the Old Level.

The line out to Ashwood Basin also saw a rapid decline in traffic. The 'country end' of the line, west of Dawley Brook, was abandoned when the National Coal

Board stopped sending coal to Ashwood for shipment to Stourport Power Station at the end of October 1953. Traffic to the landsale wharf at Dawley Brook could not save the line for long. The abandonment of that line was made very public by the demolition of the bridge over the main road at Kingswinford in April 1956. The other wharves were also closed, leading, for example, to the closure of the line up to Wellington Road, Dudley. The Wellington Road line was certainly closed by 1955 when the track was lifted leaving only a short 'stub' that served the Old Park Engineering Works.

All rail-borne coal out of Baggeridge Colliery continued to be hauled away by Pensnett Railway engines, but in about 1952 the National Coal Board introduced its own locomotives to work the line between the pit and Askew Bridge. Coal wagons were then transferred to British Railways at Baggeridge Junction, or handed over to the Pensnett engines for the remaining journey to Round Oak. At the time these were still steam-worked, but in 1962 the diesels took over this work. Four years later, on 26 September 1966, the NCB's steam locomotive handed over wagons to the Pensnett Railway's diesel for the onward journey to the steelworks for the last time. This, in effect, closed the last main line of the Pensnett Railway.

Despite the fact that this post-war period was witnessing the decline and closure of much of the Pensnett Railway, its appearance to the outside world was 'busy as usual'. This was principally because its identity as a railway was more

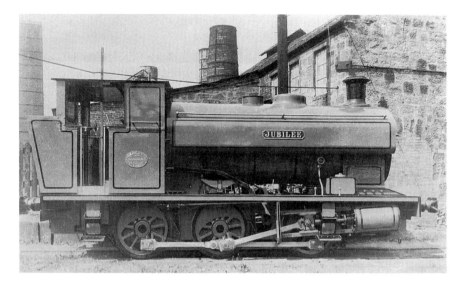

Jubilee (Andrew Barclay 2012 of 1935) as new in a smart lined-green livery – ideal for propelling heavy trains up the Barrow Hill Incline, and a survivor until 'the end of steam'. (Keith Gale Collection)

National Coal Board Hunslet 0-6-0ST No. 9 (3777 of 1952) hands over to the diesel from Round Oak (No. 10) on 26 September 1966 at Askew Bridge for the last time. This marked the closure of the line from this point back to The Wallows. (Viv Morgan Collection)

and more centred on its work as an internal system of the Round Oak Steel Works. As the running shed and maintenance workshops were at The Wallows, there was still much hustle and bustle between the worlds of the works, south of the Dudley–Brierley Hill road, and the railway to the north of that road. Modernisation of the railway in the form of dieselisation came in 1962, and a lot more 'history' was still unfolding in Round Oak Steel Works itself. The last working by a steam locomotive was at the end of June 1963.

Life Goes On at Round Oak

The Round Oak Steel Works has always been known locally as 'The Earl's', making it seem almost a personal possession of the holder of that title. All connection with the Earl of Dudley ceased in 1951 with the nationalisation of the steel industry.

Ironically, this new state of affairs did not last long. As a result of a change in government the steel industry was then denationalised in 1953, and part of the works was purchased by Tube Investments (TI). Successive waves of modernisation then took place and some of these had an impact on the railway system. For example, in 1959 a new level crossing was created lower down Level Street than the old one. This was to provide rail access to the new sidings built to serve the

Level Street Mills. Many readers will remember the distinctive level crossings of Level Street, with their lifting barriers and the cabins which overlooked them.

In 1966, as the railway was abandoning all purpose other than to be an internal works-based system, the ownership of the works was facing a new phase of ownership – a fifty-fifty partnership between Tube Investments and the state-owned British Steel Corporation.

Once again this change was followed by more plans for modernisation, although it was 1970 before these were finalised.

The changes that started in 1971 resulted in the Pensnett Railway's most iconic feature being modified. The level crossing, where the Earl's railway had crossed a main line of the national rail network since 1852, had to be realigned at quite a different angle. There were also many other modifications made to the rail network within the works.

Much money was spent rebuilding and modernising the works through the 1970s while the industry was suffering the effects of events far outside its control, making it doubtful if steel-making could ever be profitable. The Conservative Government that arrived in 1979 was prepared to take drastic action in dealing with the steel industry as a prelude to dealing with the coal industry. Annual statements made by the management at Round Oak became increasingly pessimistic and the Black Country's steel industry began to fade away.

The drama of the changing scene during the second half of the twentieth century is well represented by changes witnessed in Level Street. This 1960 view shows one of the Andrew Barclay 0-4-0STs approaching the crossing with a slag-bowl wagon. (John Dew)

Looking down Level Street in August 1970 towards the hill on the skyline topped with St Andrews Church, Netherton (compare with picture on page 101). The 'new' lower level crossing can just be located thanks to the visibility of its lifting barriers. (Viv Morgan)

A sad scene at the lower Level Street crossing in 1983, following the closure of Round Oak Steel Works. Nowadays, Level Street has become an important link between the Merry Hill shopping complex and Brierley Hill, and evidence of the crossings has disappeared. (Ned Williams)

Shunters await their fate on Kate's Bridge, August 1983. (Viv Morgan)

The 'last heat' at Round Oak was on 10 December 1982, and steel production ceased on 23 December. The works was by then wholly owned by the British Steel Corporation, which saw this closure as inevitable. All sorts of discussions were held and proposals were made right up to the last minute, but to no avail.

The Level Street Rolling Mill was greatly extended in about 1959 and this required some improved rail access. New sidings were laid and a new level crossing was installed lower down Level Street than the 'old crossing'. The crossings were fitted with lifting barriers and were controlled from distinctive cabins that soon became a feature of the Level Street scene.

What Happened Next?

The British Steel Corporation found it difficult to find a buyer for their closed and redundant steelworks; however, in June 1983 the Richardson Brothers stepped forward and bought the site. Meanwhile, the diesel locomotives that had worked on the works' system until the very end were moved from The Wallows to a siding by the late bar-finishing plant. The reclamation of the entire site was going to have to progress in stages, and 'phase one' would involve clearing the Wallows location – thus removing the last major remains of the Pensnett Railway in the form of the line's old 'works'.

Work on the Merry Hill shopping centre on land behind the site of the former steelworks produced results in 1985 when the first part of the complex opened. This area had once been mined for coal, and from the mid-nineteenth century onwards had been used as something of a 'dumping ground' for waste produced by the steelworks. Some parts of the area had been turned to pastoral agricultural use (Thomas's Farm), but other parts had been slag heaps. Even in the 1970s it had been dramatic to witness molten slag being tipped from the railway's wagons in this area.

The area occupied by the steelworks itself was a later phase in the area's redevelopment – becoming The Waterfront by 1995. Rail enthusiasts were delighted to see a monorail used briefly to link The Waterfront with the shopping complex. Meanwhile a Mr T.P. Dibdin had bought the Level Street Mills and bar-finishing plant. To everyone's amazement this led to the resurrection of three of the ex-Round Oak locomotives.

Part of the Level Street Mill and the bar-finishing building were converted into the Round Oak Rail Terminal – becoming the Steel Terminal in 1986. This has continued to develop and has changed hands a few times. New buildings were provided in 1993 despite the fact that the main-line railway passing the terminal was being closed north of Round Oak in the September of that year. Thus it is that coiled steel still arrives at Round Oak by rail and three of the ex-Pensnett Railway diesel electric locomotives still shunt railway wagons close to the site which has been at the centre of this story.

At Round Oak, and the system's extremities, the Earl of Dudley's railway made connections with the Great Western Railway. Here we see the rather nondescript setting in which the line met the GWR at Baggeridge Junction, where wagons of coal from Baggeridge Colliery could be handed over to the main-line company after only a short journey on the Earl's railway. After nationalisation of the colliery, the traffic was handled by NCB locomotives. The GWR signal box controlling this remote junction was to the left of this picture. (Viv Morgan)

Elsewhere, the route of the Pensnett Railway has been turned into a public footpath and one can now take leafy walks through Saltwells Wood or down the Barrow Hill Incline, or across the embankment between Fens Pool and Middle Pool. Other surviving elements of the Pensnett Railway will be mentioned in picture captions, but, of course, they are becoming fewer as time moves on. Recently, while walking across the embankment near the pools, I thought of Alan Hallman's description of his journey back from Dudley to Brierley Hill on the 245 bus in the 1950s. It was a journey home after an evening at Dudley Tec so it was usually dark as the bus made the slight descent from Holly Hall towards Brierley Hill. Passing Harts Hill, Alan knew just where to look right from his upstairs front seat of the bus. He could see over some rooftops to the shadowy outline of the embankment and usually he could see an engine and smoke as the last train of the day made its way back to The Wallows.

We bring our chapter devoted to those who encountered the railway as a fully operational working system, in one capacity or another, to a close, with a 'snap' taken on a box camera in the September 1932. The late Bert Bradford, of Wolverhampton, took his girlfriend for a walk in Baggeridge Woods with the intention of proposing marriage. While on the walk he was distracted by passing trains and his desire to photograph them! Above we see his picture of *Peter* – then only a 3-year-old locomotive – passing the woods with a train of coal from Baggeridge pit. Nothing could compete with the allure of the Pensnett Railway. (Bert Bradford)

2

The Kingswinford Railway

In this chapter, and the following chapters, each section of the Earl of Dudley's railway system will be described in turn. We start the tour of the system with the first part of the system to be built – the 1829 line from Shut End out to Ashwood Basin.

The line originally began from a point close to the Earl of Dudley's collieries near Corbyn's Hall – between the Dudley–Kingswinford road and Tiled House Lane. Since 1829, this area has probably been transformed several times and by the time large-scale maps of the area became available this eastern section of the line had already disappeared. Thus it is very difficult to picture this part of the system. The building of The GWR's Kingswinford Branch, the coming and going of the Stourbridge Extension Canal, and finally the arrival of the Pensnett Trading Estate, have all helped to obliterate the course of the railway.

The line must have crossed the Dudley–Kingswinford road and then curved to the west to head down a 1,000-yard incline to a location just north of St Mary's Church, Kingswinford, which became the operating centre of the system. Here it met the line into the Shut End Iron Works, developed immediately after the railway opened. Later, the line from the Himley collieries joined the main line near this point, and later still a branch to the Planet Brickworks on the Dudley–Kingswinford road also made a junction. The line ran at the back of the area which became known as The Swags, more recently landscaped as King George VI Park.

The railway maintained its westward course on the northern flank of the shallow valley of the Dawley Brook – an area now mainly covered by an industrial estate. The line was on an embankment and thus was at a suitable height to cross the Kingswinford–Wolverhampton road on an overbridge near the junction with Stallings Lane, and just north of The Bridge public house – currently still in use and retaining its name as a reminder of this landmark bridge. A branch was supplied to give access to a landsale wharf and Dawley Brook, and later this also served the gasworks.

The railway passed through Wall Heath in a very straight line to cross the main Wolverhampton–Kidderminster road (A449) by the Wall Heath Tavern.

When touring the railway with T.M. Hoskison in about 1950, Keith Gale took this picture of footplate crew and shunter working in the coal sidings at Dawley Brook. Although the line right out to Ashwood was abandoned in 1953, traffic still continued to Dawley Brook for a couple more years. The gasworks was built in about 1870 and made good use of the Pensnett Railway's Ashwood line, independently of the landsale wharf next door. (Keith Gale)

One old photograph of the Congregational church shows the rails emerging from Foundry Road, but a picture of a train crossing the main road has remained elusive. A line of trees lining the recreation ground identifies the one-time course of the line, but once again modern housing has successfully obscured the railway's passage until we catch a glimpse of bridge abutments on Swindon Road. At one time there were sidings into sand-holes on this stretch – another source of traffic for the railway. The embankment now forms a boundary of the rugby club's ground, and its former course can also be seen from the sports ground on the Mile Flat.

When first built, the railway descended another cable-worked incline to makes its way to the terminus at Ashwood Basin. Later trains were able to ascend and descend this incline without assistance and all traces of the one-time engine house have disappeared. Once at the basin, the line divided so that access was provided to both sides of the canal and to a pier which enabled wagons to discharge their load directly into narrowboats below. Today it is difficult to imagine that the marina was once a busy interchange between railway and canal.

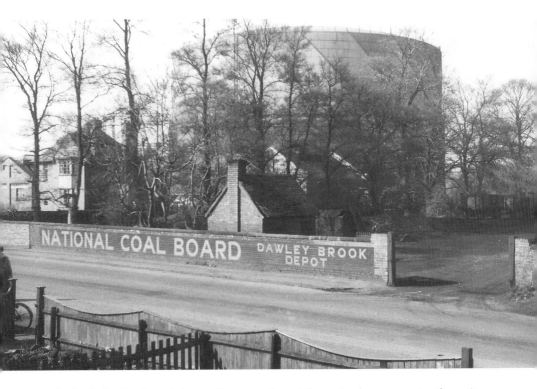

The landsale wharf was between the gasworks and the embankment carrying the main running line of the Ashwood Branch, as it later became known. The nationalisation of the coal industry led to some repainting of this wall – all of which has disappeared, although the manager's house at the gasworks has survived. (Keith Gale)

The bridge carrying the railway over the Kingswinford–Wolverhampton road was quite substantial and included a pedestrian arch in the abutment on the right. This picture shows that the word 'Baggeridge' had been painted out during the war, although people were still exhorted to 'buy coal'. (Keith Gale)

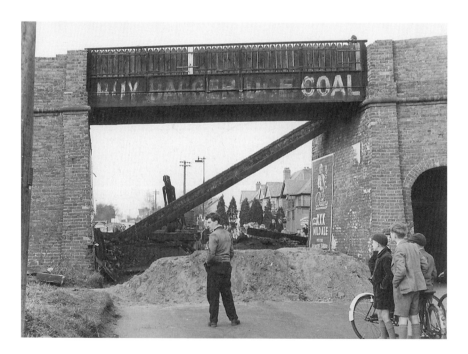

The bridge at Dawley Brook being demolished on September 1956, a year after the last trains had run to the Dawley Brook Wharf – by then 'NCB'. (Keith Gale Collection)

A pre-war photograph taken at Ashwood shows sidings on both sides of the basin as well as two lines on the timber pier. (Vic Smallshire Collection)

A 1920s picture shows the amount of physical labour used in transferring coal to canal boat, and a dumb-buffered wagon still is use. A number of men were employed by the railway to deal with traffic at Ashwood Basin at the time. (Keith Hodgkins Collection)

The weighbridge office at Ashwood Basin was a typical Pensnett Railway structure complete with 'EoD' plaque in the end gable. Lower Ashwood Lane is beyond the fence and the viaduct across the basin is to the right. (Viv Morgan)

Ashwood Cottage. The 1901 census tells us that this house was tenanted by William George and his family. He is described as a 'coal loader' and ten years later he is described as a 'coal porter'. His sons, William and Alfred, were born in the cottage and joined the railway as platelayers and graduated to the footplate. (Peter George)

J.T. Price's Planet brickyard was served by a wharf at right angles to the main Kingswinford–Dudley road, and was still seeing occasional use in 1950 when photographed by Keith Gale. (Keith Gale)

One of the Pensnett Railway's 0-4-0STs shunts the sidings at the Planet Brickworks in the 1920s. Locomotives sent out to shunt wagons at Baggeridge Colliery often undertook a trip down the line to Ashwood and shunted wagons at this wharf and at Dawley Brook as required. Beyond the works it is possible to make out the cliff at the back of the company's marl hole – some of which still exists today. (Ron Workman Collection)

3

The Main Line

What became the main line of the Pensnett Railway was not planned as such – it simply became the main line by virtue of the fact that it linked the two principal locations associated with the Earl of Dudley's industrial activities: the works at Round Oak and Baggeridge Colliery reached via a twentieth-century addition to the system.

Once the railway had passed under the main Dudley–Brierley Hill road just north of the Round Oak works, it entered an area called The Wallows. Many small pits had operated in this area in a Wallows' 'series'. These had first been served by rail as a result of building one of the lines recommended by Mackelcan in 1843. The upper line, as it was once known, ran in one direction to Nine Locks pit in Mill Street, Brierley Hill, and in the other direction to The Wallows, where it met Lord Ward's canal. The latter was built from the Dudley Canal near Parkhead to The Wallows and opened in 1840.

The Wallows started to become home to engine sheds and light repair facilities from about 1903 onwards but became the full operational and maintenance centre of the railway system from 1926 once the Castle Mill Works was closed. In the nineteenth century, The Wallows was important in terms of the canal basin, and as a 'jumping off point' from which to extend the railway up towards the Earl's Himley Coalfield. To reach the latter, the railway had to make its way northwards to Pensnett, originally by skirting Fens Pool on its eastern shore and after 1883 via an embankment between Middle Pool and Fens Pool, the reservoirs that fed the Stourbridge Canal. There was a short incline before reaching the embankment, but this was only worked by a stationary engine for a very short time. North of Pensnett, the railway did have to include a lengthy and steepish incline to descend Barrow Hill, but from 1921 onwards, even this could be locomotive worked.

At the foot of the Barrow Hill Incline there was a short branch to Old Park Colliery No. 58 and later a brickyard. Later, this area was also the scene of a junction with another private railway built in 1899 to serve Gibbons' Dibdale Brickworks. The main line curved westwards and formed a loop between

Coopers Bank Road and Sandfield Bridge on Cinder Road. A footbridge crossed the loop, connecting Chase Road and Smithy Lane, and this can be seen in many photographs of this part of the line. An engine shed was also provided at this point, but was abandoned in the late 1920s when The Wallows became the system's locomotive shed.

Beyond Sandfield Road Bridge, the railway entered an area inhabited by the pits in the Himley Colliery 'series'. However, before reaching that point the line was provided with yet another loop. Beyond the loop, the main line passed under the northernmost part of the GWR Kingswinford Branch heading for Askew

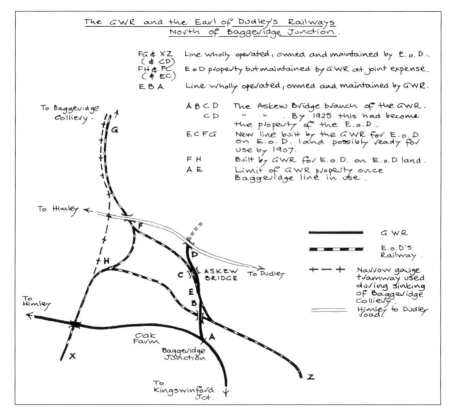

This diagram of the various lines in the Baggeridge Junction/Askew Bridge area includes the narrow gauge line built to assist the shaft construction at Baggeridge Colliery, and the short narrow gauge line north of the Dudley–Himley road (shown by a double dotted line) that ran briefly to Straits Green Colliery. The former met the Pensnett Railway at Himley No. 5 pit, close to the point marked 'H'. In the centre of this area is the Glynne Arms, better known today as The Crooked House. Anyone taking the narrow lane from Himley Road down to this pub is very aware of passing through bridges that once carried the Baggeridge line and the old main line of the Pensnett Railway.

Bridge and reached some of the Himley pits. A sharp curve from the loop also provided the link between the Pensnett Railway and the GWR's Askew Bridge branch, which was introduced in 1875. A further development came in 1906 when construction of the line from here to Baggeridge Colliery began.

The Baggeridge Colliery line, built by the GWR, was completed by 1910 but did not really come into use until 1912 when the pit began production. The GWR's motive for offering to build the line to their standards was that coal would also be able reach their lines by exiting at what became Baggeridge Junction.

ROUND OAK STEEL WKS L^{TD}
PENSNETT RAILWAY
PROPERTY

A general view of The Wallows on 2 May 1959. The basin at the end of Lord Ward's canal (aka the Pensnett Canal) is now out of use and the wagons by the crane are loaded with scrap metal for the furnaces rather than coal for transhipment. On the left are the railway's works and running sheds. In the centre of the picture, in a slight cutting, is the main running line that we will now follow as we imagine a journey up to Baggeridge Colliery. (P.J. Shoesmith)

As the Pensnett Railway's main line left The Wallows it traversed this embankment between Middle Pool and Fens Pool, seen on the right. In the distance is the township of Pensnett, and on the horizon, on the right, is Barrow Hill. (Michael Hale)

If all this sounds complicated, it only gets worse! In 1865, a way of linking the Pensnett Railway with the Kingswinford Railway was found. This involved extending the main line from Himley Colliery No. 4 westwards and then southwards until reaching the original railway of 1829 at a point near existing junctions just north of Kingswinford Church. This link transformed the railways into a single unified system, from then on known as the Pensnett Railway. (The western portion of the Kingswinford Railway then became the Ashwood Branch of the Pensnett Railway.)

One further link was added to make it possible for trains from Baggeridge Colliery to run directly to the Ashwood Branch. Meanwhile, to make our way up the Baggeridge line we have to climb steadily towards a bridge under the Dudley–Himley road at a place called High Arcal. At this point the railway was running within the boundary of his lordship's estate at Himley Hall. This became the terminus for the passenger trains associated with the fetes at Himley Hall from 1929 to 1938. The railway ran through wooded countryside until suddenly arriving at Baggeridge Colliery, the northernmost outpost of the system.

The bridge over Queen Street looking towards Commonside carried a 'Low Bridge' warning. The bridge showed signs of having been rebuilt at various times and had no parapet on the other side. It has long since been demolished, but traces of the embankment can still be seen. The track between Pensnett and Round Oak was unofficially very much used as a public footpath – which is what it has now become. (Viv Morgan)

Jeremy (Andrew Barclay 1965 of 1927) stands by the southern portal of the bridge under the Dudley–Kingswinford road at Pensnett on 30 May 1951. A stationary engine house at this location once provided cable haulage for trains climbing the Barrow Hill Incline to this point. (A.W. Croughton)

From the parapet of the overbridge carrying the Dudley–Kingswinford road at Pensnett, it was possible to take in this view of the Barrow Hill Incline. The trackbed has now become a public footpath and the vegetation on either side has grown considerably. (Viv Morgan)

A loaded train leaves Coopers Bank to begin the ascent of the Barrow Hill Incline in June 1951. Trains were usually 'propelled' up the incline and 'led' down it. Even so, runaways were not unknown and catch points were installed at the foot of the incline to derail runaways. (A.W. Claughton)

As the railway began to curve to the north-west, it entered an area between Coopers Bank Road and Cinder Road where there were loops and sidings, and at one time an engine shed. The location is often recognised in photographs by the presence of the footbridge seen here, which carried a footpath from Smithy Lane to Chase Road. *Queen Elizabeth* and *Lady Morvyth* bask in the evening sunlight sometime in 1952. (Tim Shuttleworth)

Yorkshire Engine 0-4-0 diesel No.10 pauses at Coopers Bank on 26 September 1966 on the last day that coal was being despatched from Baggeridge to Round Oak. (Viv Morgan Collection)

Just before passing under Cinder Road at Sandfield Bridge, watering facilities were provided as seen in this early 1950s view. (A.W. Croughton/Keith Gale)

Duchess of Gloucester (Andrew Barclay 2110 of 1941) pauses at this location sometime in 1952. (Tim Shuttleworth)

Yorkshire Engine 0-4-0 diesel No. 9 heads through Sandfield Bridge in 1966 – by which time the cottage adjoining the line (71 Cinder Bank) had been much rebuilt. (Dudley Archives)

Once beyond Sandfield Bridge the railway comes to another centre of activity. Once again there are loops – both occupied with wagons in this 1952 photograph. Just above the second wagon from the right it is possible to see more wagons on the curve that takes the railway up to Askew Bridge sidings and on to the line to Baggeridge Colliery. On the left of the picture is the double-line overbridge that carries the GWR's Askew Bridge branch. 'Straight ahead' the main line heads on to the pits of the Himley Coalfield and eventually on to the 1865 'link' that unified the separate components of the system. (Tim Shuttleworth)

The important curve referred to above can be seen more clearly in the background of this picture taken on 19 April 1952. Andrew Barclay 0-6-0ST *Duchess of Gloucester* occupies the foreground. (Tim Shuttleworth)

A 'runaway' of loaded coal wagons has left Baggeridge Colliery and run down the line only to derail on the sharp inclined curve described on the previous page. (The main line can be seen at a lower level on the right.) The accident happened on 29 June 1964 and, as in other similar incidents, it was seen as curious that these events happened at night and by morning vast quantities of coal had disappeared from the scene. (Viv Morgan Collection)

NCB Hunslet 0-6-0ST No. 8 seen on the GWR Askew Bridge branch overbridge in 1963, by which time the track on the Pensnett Railway main line seems to have been lifted, leaving a pile of chairs and sleepers in the left-hand corner of the picture. (Paul Dorney)

The bridge seen in the previous picture is seen again here in 1951. It is not clear how much the line beyond this point was used in later years. Coal from Baggeridge Colliery to Ashwood Basin was able to reach its destination via a direct line put in during the GWR's building of the Baggeridge branch, and the pits of the Himley Coalfield had closed by the time this picture was taken. (Keith Gale)

Wagons were still to be found at Himley Colliery No. 4 when Keith Gale took this picture in 1950, and the main line in the foreground still looks distinctly 'in use', perhaps because it was still the direct route to Ashwood and Dawley Brook. No. 4 was the largest pit in the Himley series, and although 'worked out' by the 1930s, the screens here were brought back into use for processing coal that was brought here from small local pits that were revived as part of the war effort. (Keith Gale)

Returning to the Baggeridge Colliery line, this picture shows the railway climbing towards the pit at the point where it passes under the Dudley–Himley road. This was sometimes known locally as the Yellow Bridge. Interestingly, this 1963 picture shows the direct line at Ashwood coming in on the left – very overgrown and used in places as a derelict wagon store! After Baggeridge Colliery closed in 1968, the trackbed seen here was converted into a private unsurfaced road used by heavy lorries bringing marl up to Baggeridge Brickworks for a time. The bridge has now lost its parapets and the area behind the photographer has been very heavily landscaped. (Keith Gale)

Queen Elizabeth propels a train of 'empties' back up to Baggeridge Colliery on 8 June 1951 – passing through the area known as High Arcal, with the Yellow Bridge just discernible in the background. (A.W. Croughton/Phil Jones)

An NCB Hunslet 0-6-0ST descends the bank at High Arcal in about 1965 with a loaded train. The NCB also seemed to favour working these trains with a brake van, unlike Pensnett Railway practices. (Michael Hale)

A fairly new Andrew Barclay 0-4-0ST is seen shunting the sidings at Baggeridge Colliery in this picture taken in the interwar period. The line in the left-hand foreground of the picture went round to a landsale wharf. Baggeridge Colliery became operational in 1912 and was worked until March 1968, having become part of the National Coal Board in 1947. From 1952 onwards the NCB provided its own locomotives (two Hunslet 0-6-0STs) to work between Baggeridge and Askew Bridge/Baggeridge Junction. (BCS Collection)

The tracks at Baggeridge Colliery seen in 1963. On the right, the railway's weighbridge and office are located just beyond a typical Earl of Dudley water tower. Beyond the weighbridge office we can see the very plain rectangular engine shed that the NCB built in 1952 to house their Hunslet 0-6-0STs that took over working the line from the Pensnett Railway engines. (Viv Morgan)

Hunslet 0-6-0ST (3777 of 1952) NCB No. 9 stands at Baggeridge Colliery with a brake van in about 1967 when coal was only being despatched via the railway to the exchange point with British Railways at Baggeridge Junction. (Paul Dorney)

NCB Hunslet 0-6-0ST No. 8 pauses at the water tower just south of the weighbridge at Baggeridge Colliery. The water tank was similar to others used all over the Pensnett Railway system but was something of an anachronism as far as the colliery was concerned. The pit used water drawn from within the mine itself, but this was too 'hard' for locomotive use and therefore South Staffordshire Water Company had to be paid to supply this tank. (Vic Smallshire)

Hunslet 0-6-0ST No. 8 arrives at Baggeridge Colliery with a train of empty wagons in a picture which reinforces the impression that the approach to the colliery was very rural. (Vic Smallshire)

Once the branch to Baggeridge Colliery came into full use in 1912 it rather dominated everyone's perception of the Pensnett Railway, but it has to be remembered that the main line was really the 1865 link that continued westward from the Askew Bridge area, passed the location of Himley No. 4 pit and then turned south-westwards, passing the location of Himley No. 5 pit and Himley No. 7. The line also passed under the GWR's extension of their original Kingswinford Branch on its way out to Himley, Wombourn etc. (Construction started in 1913, the line opened in 1925, and closed in 1965.) This 1986 picture shows the trackbed of the old main line just north of Oak Lane as it passes under the GWR. (Ned Williams)

Looking in the other direction, in 1950, we see the long loop, crossed by Oak Lane, and wagons of coke being unloaded. There had been coke ovens in this area, and a loading platform on this side of Oak Lane. (Keith Gale)

This water tower stood on the 1865 link between Oak Lane and Stallings Lane near the site of Himley No. 8 pit and was dismantled in August 1950, five months after this picture was taken. It was replaced with a new galvanised square tank. (Keith Gale)

The 'beehive' crossing keeper's shelter adjoined the point where the Pensnett Railway crossed Stallings Lane. Keith Gale photographed it in April 1950 and in his notes referred to it as 'Bottle Lodge'. Above the door is an 'E.D. – 1870' plaque. After the war, trains were so infrequent it must have been quite a boring job! (Keith Gale)

0-6-0ST *Jubilee* begins to propel the wagons from Askew Bridge into the exchange sidings where they can await transfer to a Western Region BR train in April 1950, two years prior to the NCB taking responsibility for this out-going coal traffic. (Keith Gale)

4

The Dudley Branch

The Dudley Branch of the Pensnett Railway grew out of the development of the system following the Mackelcan recommendations of the 1840s. In anticipation of the development of the works at Round Oak, in the 1850s, it was seen that coal from the Earl of Dudley's pits in the Oak Farm series could also benefit from being transported either to The Wallows canal basin, or to the existing ironworks around the eastern end of Brierley Hill.

A line was built from The Wallows that circled the eastern shore of Fens Pool. Not far from The Wallows a junction was put in and a line headed in a more north-easterly direction, running parallel to what is now North View Drive. By the time the line was passing the little community of Low Town it was heading directly northwards, and just before passing under the Dudley–Kingswinford road there was a loop and weighbridge provided. This area seems to have been the 'High Lanes' referred to by Mackelcan. In later years this patch was dominated by the Old Park Engineering Works (later Simon Engineering, now Essar Steels), and in the 1960s this was the terminus of the line. Originally the branch dived under the Dudley–Kingswinford road, at a point now obscured by the island at the gateway to Russells Hall Hospital. One of the Earl of Dudley's 'estate houses' was built by the bridge and was once occupied by the Mantle family.

Once north of the Dudley–Kingswinford road, the railway was in the area known as the Old Park. It originally turned slightly to the west and terminated at the area now just behind Russells Hall Hospital. So far, the account of the Pensnett Railway serving this area has been relatively unchronicled, but once the extension was made towards Dudley in the 1860s we are on better-known territory. For example, the opening of the line right through to Wellington Road Wharf in Dudley can be quoted as occuring exactly 1 November 1865.

It is impossible to account for all the lines extended to various pits in the Old Park Coalfield, but the line to Dudley skirted the area by keeping fairly close to the Dudley–Kingswinford road and passed through Scotts Green and Springs Mire to reach Wellington Road just south of the New Dock.

At Wellington Road, the line divided into two sidings and the usual office and weighbridge completed the facilities. A feature of the wall site was that just before reaching the wharf, the line passed under a footbridge carrying a footpath that linked the hamlet of Springs Mire with the New Dock. This footbridge, like the one at Coopers Bank, shows an intriguing concern on the part of the Pensnett Railway for established rights of way. Other interesting aspects of the branch include the fact that the buffer stops at Wellington Road were almost directly above the Dudley Canal Tunnel, of 1892 vintage, and the route taken to reach Wellington Road formed a southern boundary to the original Dudley Golf Course.

Like all branches of the Pensnett Railway, the Dudley Branch also spawned further branches and spurs. One served the Hope Iron Works at Scotts Green, and another served the Electrical Generating Station at Springs Mire. The latter belonged to the Shropshire, Worcestershire & Staffordshire Electric Power Company, and the building, at the end of Bull Street, surprisingly survives to this day. Another spur ran across the Kingswinford and Stourbridge roads on the level virtually at the point where they diverge. To do so, the Pensnett Railway's tracks must have crossed the rails of the local tramway system on both roads and it is a pity that none of this seems to have been photographed.

The Wellington Road Wharf appears to have closed in 1955, after which the branch was cut back to the south of the Dudley–Kingswinford road at the Old Park Engineering Works.

This photograph was taken in 1970 on the section of the Pensnett Railway's Dudley Branch just as it curves northwards to pass the little hamlet of Low Town – a small colliers' village that was built in the first half of the nineteenth century to house men who worked in the pits of the Old Park. Uralia Films were shooting a film called *You've Seen It All Before* and the heroine, Jean Preston, was about to be tied to the rails before the arrival of an important express train. In reality, the occasional one-wagon train sent to collect scrap from the Old Park Engineering Works had already ceased running. The iron railings on the right once encircled sidings that had been laid alongside the branch to cope with storing incoming coal to Round Oak during the Second World War. (Ned Williams)

Thomas Michael Hoskison stands on the footplate of Andrew Barclay 0-6-0ST (2014 of 1937) *Queen Elizabeth* in February 1951 just before he and Keith Gale travel over the Dudley Branch of the Pensnett Railway. (Keith Gale)

In February 1951, Keith Gale took this photograph from the footplate of *Queen Elizabeth* as it propelled empty coal trucks back to The Wallows from Dudley's Wellington Road Wharf. On the left are the houses of Kingswinford Road and the junction with Hilderic Crescent, on the right are the wastelands of the Old Park – now covered with houses of the Russells Hall Estate. Note the brakeman travelling at the front end of the train. (Keith Gale)

A.W. Croughton inspected the Dudley Branch on 30 May 1951 and stood at the location seen above in Keith Gale's photograph. Andrew Barclay 0-6-0ST (2110 of 1941) *Duchess of Gloucester* is propelling loaded wagons towards Wellington Road Wharf. Barrow Hill can be seen on the horizon on the left of the picture. Just beyond the engine one can see what a wasteland the Old Park had become. (A.W. Croughton)

At the entrance to Wellington Road Wharf the lines divided to create two sidings and passed under the footbridge carrying the footpath from Springs Mire to Waterloo Terrace in the New Dock, as seen in this 1951 view. (Keith Gale)

Wellington Road Wharf, Dudley on 30 May 1951. *Duchess of Gloucester* had just dropped the loaded wagons in the siding on the right and is about to depart with the empties. Note 'The Earl of Dudley's Arms' in the background – since replaced with a more modern building on the opposite side of Wellington Road. To the left it is possible to see the gable end of St Luke's Church – since demolished. Today, few people realise that the Earl of Dudley's railway once came so close to the centre of Dudley, and coal merchants in Wellington Road could receive coal directly from the pit by rail. (A.W. Croughton)

The usual weighbridge and office were to be found at Wellington Road, and in this case the plaque in the gable end was dated 1864 and featured a coronet rather than the initials of the mineral agent. Note the absence of proper buffer stops at the end of the siding. No sign of the yard can be seen today. (Keith Gale)

Yorkshire Engine Co. diesel electric 0-4-0 No. 3 makes a solitary last trip to the buffer stop forming the end of the Old Park Branch – the last remnant of the line to Dudley – in about 1974. (Gordon Nutt)

5

A Narrow Gauge Diversion

In order to facilitate the sinking of the shafts at Baggeridge Colliery, a narrow gauge railway was built northwards from Himley Pit No. 5 up to the site of the future colliery. This route was slightly to the west of the line used by the standard gauge line built for access to the colliery by the GWR, although worked as part of the Pensnett Railway. The narrow gauge line must have been limited in the size and quantity of materials it could have carried. The gauge was 2ft 6in and at least two locomotives are known to have worked on it.

This picture is dated August 1901 and we are told it was taken by the Wishing Pool in Baggeridge Wood. It appears to show an 0-6-0 well tank known as *Doctor Jim*, possibly built by the Lilleshall Co. (Keith Gale)

In this case the locomotive seems to one of the three 0-4-0STs built at the Castle Mill Works, and used on pit tramways. (Jim Evans Collection)

6

The Saltwells Branch

The expansion of the Pensnett Railway in the mid-nineteenth century also saw the lines extend into the area to the south of Round Oak, into the Saltwells Coalfield. To reach this area another incline had to be built taking the railway from the point where it joined the upper line near Level Street, close to the Level New Furnaces, to the point where the railway could dive beneath the Dudley–Worcester turnpike road – in this stretch known as Pedmore Road. The incline became known as the Tipsyford Incline and the overbridge became known as the Tipsyford Bridge. (The Tipsyford Brook drained the basin between Round Oak and Quarry Bank that is today occupied by the Merry Hill shopping complex.)

Immediately south of Level Street the lines of the Pensnett Railway divided. The right-hand line was the branch to the Nine Locks Iron Works and Saltwells No. 29 pit, at Mill Street. To the left, the railway began the 1 in 40 descent of the Tipsyford Incline. The stationary engine had its back to Level Street and faced straight down the incline. Wagons made their way up and down the incline as one might expect, but locomotives had to do the same to access the Saltwells branches, and occasionally the cable was used to assist locomotive-hauled wagons.

A little way down the incline a siding providing reverse access to the Old Level Iron Works was absorbed into the Round Oak works in the 1890s, although on the 'other side' of the canal. At the foot of the incline a lengthy branch ran round to sidings on a site now buried beneath the Merry Hill shopping complex. From the sidings, a narrow gauge tramway ran up to Saltwells Pit No. 35, now buried beneath the Shaw-Hellier Estate.

Reversing off loops at the foot of the incline was another engine shed used to house a locomotive working the Saltwells lines until such matters were centralised at The Wallows. The bridge under the Pedmore Road was narrow like so many on the Pensnett Railway, but once through the bridge the railway became quite 'rural' as it made its way through Saltwells Wood. Not far into the wood another junction was provided when a branch was built to serve Saltwells Pit No. 33 at Quarry Bank. The branch traversed the wood and crossed Coppice Lane on the level not far from the Tin Tabernacle (now Birch Coppice Methodist Church).

The branch continued in a southerly direction via the Coppice until reaching the pit. The pit probably started work in the early 1890s and was closed in 1912, so the branch was short-lived.

The main line of the Saltwells system also continued on its way through Saltwells Wood and passed just behind the Saltwells Inn. The saltwater spa itself had been nearby at the confluence of the Tipsyford Brook and the Black Brook. The bath was last used in the 1930s and all remains of it were swept away in the early 1970s by the Severn Trent Water Authority. However the trackbed of the railway survives as an attractive footpath through the woods.

At the location of Saltwells Pit No. 31 there was an important junction. One line carried on straight ahead in an easterly direction all the way to the main road between Netherton and Old Hill, serving sidings to Saltwells Nos 19 and 20 on the way. The Pensnett Railway crossed Bowling Green Road and the Dudley–Old Hill turnpike road on the level – the latter involving crossing tracks of the local tramway. Ultimately the line halted at Saltwells Pit No. 28, but was probably more used to reach yet another landsale wharf established on the Saltwells side of the main road.

At Saltwells Pit No. 1, a branch deviated and ascended an incline to Saltwells Pits Nos 5 and 6, which were alongside Saltwells Basin on the Dudley No. 2 Canal. Messrs Hoskison and Gale described this as Primrose Basin which it was not! Primrose Basin, with no rail access, was a little further along the canal opposite Lloyd's Proving House. It was a LNWR-owned basin – later LMS – but had nothing to do with the Pensnett Railway. The 'true record' is that the incline and Saltwells Basin were brought into use on 27 July 1853.

At Saltwells Junction – i.e. at the one-time location of Pit No. 1 – a line turned south-eastwards and, after emerging from the wood, crossed Coppice Lane/Saltwells Road on the level. Just before the level crossing, a facility was built for processing slag which became known as The Earl's Muck Works. Today one makes one's way up the side of these works to gain access to the Saltwells Inn.

Not long after crossing Saltwells Road the railway passed through the hamlet of Mushroom Green and passed Saltwells Pit No. 25 which was on top of a mound that still exists today by Quarry Road. The railway's passage through Mushroom Green was fascinating and included a level crossing – the crossing keeper's 'lookout' still visible in an existing building. Alan Hallman, a Pensnett Railway 'enthusiast', recalls that his first wife, Joy, used to take her father's tea to the Saltwells Road level crossing. Her father, Horace Philpott, was a driver on the Pensnett Railway, and he often gave Joy a ride on the footplate when she arrived with his tea, but these trips only took her as far as Mushroom Green.

While running parallel to Quarry Road, the railway came to yet another junction. At this point a branch went forward across Quarry Road at the junction with Dudley Wood Road, and headed for the Providence Iron Works in Old Hill.

The works belonged to Joseph Penn who first requested a branch in 1884. It was constructed in 1892 and added another ½ mile to the Pensnett Railway network. A famous boiler explosion at Penn's works in 1906 brought attention to the place and it hit the headlines again when wagons ran away and derailed in the works' yard in 1937.

The Saltwells main line then swung past Saltwells Pit No. 24 and headed for Forge Lane, Cradley Heath. To do so, it crossed part of the site of the Cradley Pool and had sidings into Saltwells Pit No. 30. Just to the north of Forge Lane it opened into a fan of sidings and another landsale wharf. These sidings were adjacent to an area where the old Cradley Pool had been drained and sewerage pipes had been built and then buried on their way from Quarry Bank (Cradley Forge) and Cradley Heath. The Pipes, as the area was called, was something of a local 'monkey run', and during the day was an adventure playground for local children. Some children ventured into the sidings and played among the wagons. Inevitably there were accidents and one incident led to the death of a local lad who was playing between wagons as they began to move.

The terminus of the Saltwells Branch was the landsale wharf on the north side of Forge Lane, but as from April 1862 onwards, the GWR's Stourbridge Extension line came to Cradley and Cradley Heath station a few yards from Forge Lane. A connection was thus made with the GWR by taking the Pensnett Railway across Forge Lane and into the goods yard on the GWR. This was completed in 1874 – a year before the connection with the GWR at Askew Bridge was opened.

In conclusion, it is obvious that the Saltwells network was an extensive section of the Pensnett Railway, although less well known and recorded compared with the lines north of Round Oak. Its decline and demise was fairly rapid after the Second World War, and the whole line from the bottom of Tipsyford to Cradley Heath was already closed when T.M. Hoskison started writing up the railway's history in 1951.

The top of the Tipsyford Incline looking towards Level Street – just outside the right-hand side of the photograph. We are looking straight towards the engine house. The stationary engine was probably built at the Earl of Dudley's Castle Mill Works and was similar to colliery winding engines produced there. In front of the engine house are the lines that once formed the Nine Locks Branch. (Viv Morgan)

Andrew Barclay 0-4-0ST (2054 of 1938) *Lady Morvyth* ascends the Tipsyford Incline with cable assistance. The wagons are carrying bars from the Level Street Rolling Mills and the lower section of the incline may have been out of use at this time. (Viv Morgan)

Looking down the Tipsyford Incline after its abandonment. Saltwells Wood can be seen on the horizon. There was quite an art in working this incline. The winder could cause descending trucks to buck slightly as they reached the bottom of the incline and this would enable a man to deftly remove the pin in the draw shackle, and the released trucks would roll clear of the incline with their own momentum. The rope would then be attached to the three or four trucks waiting to ascend the incline. Sometimes a train and engine would want to ascend the incline but the rope was at the top. The crew would go to the Saltwells Weighbridge office and phone the winder. When the engine gave two blasts on the whistle the winder would send the rope down the incline with a couple of empty wagons. (Keith Gale)

The locomotive shed at the foot of the Tipsyford Incline was looking very abandoned and derelict by 1951. It had once been home to engines allocated to working the Saltwells lines. (Keith Gale)

The loop just behind the Saltwells Inn, looking very abandoned in 1951. Just beyond the water tower in the distance the lines diverged: one line went straight ahead to the Netherton–Old Hill road and Saltwells Basin, the other went to Cradley Heath via Mushroom Green. (Keith Gale)

Some wagons bask in the sunshine alongside the slag-processing facility or 'muck works' just north of Saltwells Road on the line to Cradley Heath in 1951. This space now provides road access to the Saltwells Inn. (Keith Gale)

In 1951, Keith Gale photographed one of the Constable & Hart wagons still to be found at the 'muck works' by Saltwells Road. The firm was established in 1903 centred around quarrying in Derbyshire but later spread across the Midlands in the roadstone and tarmacadam business. (Keith Gale)

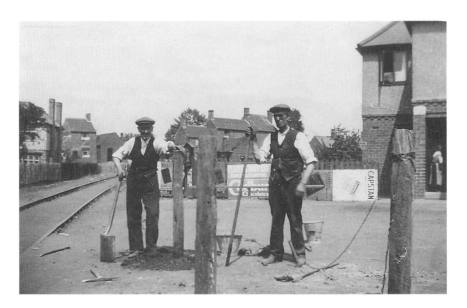

On the left of this picture we see the rails of the Cradley Heath branch of the Pensnett Railway as it makes its way through Mushroom Green. Jasper's shop can be seen on the right, and Emma Jasper stands in the doorway. (Julie Tonkin Collection)

The Saltwells Branch ended at this landsale wharf on the northern side of Forge Lane, Cradley Heath, where the usual weighbridge and office were provided, in the shadow of the 'pit bonks' of Saltwells Pit No. 30. It is interesting to note that the wharf itself is numbered '30', reflecting its proximity to that pit rather than the actual number of landsale wharves on the Pensnett Railway. (Keith Gale Collection)

The same weighbridge office and yard entrance can be seen in this photograph taken in 1951 looking in the opposite direction. A track was extended across the Forge Lane in 1874 to make a connection with the GWR's Stourbridge Extension line by sweeping into the main-line company's goods yard at the far end of the goods shed seen in the centre of the picture. The Midland Red bus garage on the left of the picture will help readers get their bearings. (Keith Gale)

A well-known picture of Joseph Penn's Providence Iron Works after the boiler explosion of 4 July 1906. Pensnett Railway wagons, some still full of coal, have been derailed and scattered around the yard. Three people died as a result of the explosion. There was another incident at the Providence Iron Works in January 1939 when two wagons coming into the yard over the weighbridge derailed and crashed into the office building and demolished it! Frank Maley who worked as a clerk in the office had a miraculous escape. He usually left the office as soon as he heard the whistle of an approaching train, but on this occasion stopped to deal with a phone call and was not standing by the weighbridge at the critical moment. (Viv Morgan Collection)

Today the Pensnett Railway's line through Saltwells Wood survives as a footpath, and in 2012 this sculpture by Luke Perry appeared on the trackbed. The legend on the tender implies that trains traversed this part of the system as late as the 1960s. In fact it was an early 'casualty' and trains had ceased running through these woods in 1950. (John James)

7

Around The Wallows

The area just to the north of the Dudley–Brierley Hill road is known as The Wallows, and it eventually found itself to be very much at the centre of the Pensnett Railway. As a potential coal-producing area very close to the ironworks in the Brierley Hill area, it was mined fairly early on in the development of the Earl's interests, and a number of pits were eventually numbered in a Wallows series. Of course these became worked out, and by 1900 the remaining workings were renumbered in the Himley and Saltwells series.

Mackelcan's proposals of 1843 suggested a railway be built stretching from Nine Locks Iron Works and the adjoining pit (later known as Saltwells No. 29) through Round Oak, out to The Wallows, where it would meet the basin at the end of Lord Ward's canal of 1839, and on the High Lanes. As described elsewhere, this line found itself crossing the Oxford, Worcester and Wolverhampton Railway's main line, as well as having to pass beneath the Dudley–Kingswinford road.

The principal feature of The Wallows area for many years was the canal basin at the end of Lord Ward's canal, but from 1926 onwards it became the operational and maintenance centre of the railway following the demise of the Castle Mill Works over on the far side of Dudley. The works developed to the point where major repairs could be undertaken, and later still they looked after the fleet of diesel locomotives. A facility for wagon maintenance and repair was also developed at The Wallows. Everything came to an end at The Wallows with the closure of the steelworks in 1983.

The track layout at The Wallows changed considerably over the years. In the early days it was centred on providing sidings on either side of the canal basin. Later sidings were provided as stabling for traffic coming to the centre of the system from its outposts, and for marshalling empty wagons for their next journey. At one stage, a landsale wharf operated not far from The Wallows, known as The Terrace. At the end of the railway's life, sidings near The Wallows became the last resting place for ex-main-line railway stock about to be reduced to scrap metal.

People remember The Wallows as a fan of railway lines, a variety of sheds, and the glimpse of locomotives coming and going. This picture captures the atmosphere of The Wallows as it was in about 1960. (Jim Houghton)

The canal basin at The Wallows once provided an outlet for coal brought to this point by the various lines of the Pensnett Railway, and incoming material could arrive here in the form of ironstone. After the Second World War the basin was used less and less – as seen in the later photograph reproduced on page 52. (Keith Gale Collection)

During the final years of steam operation, photographers were drawn to The Wallows to capture the atmosphere of a busy independent industrial railway. *Lady Edith* (Andrew Barclay 2117 of 1941) survived until the end of steam, and is seen here taking water at The Wallows from one of the standard Earl of Dudley's tanks. (Dudley Archives)

A hazy summer day at The Wallows – 1 June 1951: *Duchess of Kent* (Andrew Barclay 0-4-0ST 2007 of 1935) stands in front of an open wagon and *Jubilee* (Andrew Barclay 2012 of 1935) as men and wheelbarrow complete the composition. Behind *Jubilee* is a large shed called The Hippodrome, as it was built in 1938, the same year as Dudley Hippodrome. (A.W. Croughton, via Phil Jones)

The Hippodrome is still visible in this photograph taken on Whit Monday – 27 May 1980 – as Yorkshire Engine Co. 0-4-0 diesels congregate. Behind No. 3 is the running shed, and behind No. 10, on the right, is the wagon repair shop. The locomotives carried a bright yellow and black striped livery to aid visibility and originally had phosphor bronze bells with a very melodious clang! (Gordon Nutt)

Yorkshire Engine 0-4-0 diesel electric No. 4 (2774 of 1959) up on the jacks in The Hippodrome while undergoing repair on 8 November 1977. This engine survived to be taken into the stock of Round Oak Rail, which still operate a steel terminal at Round Oak. (Gordon Nutt)

Yorkshire Engine diesel electric 0-4-0s receiving attention on 9 July 1978. (No. 3 – 2662 of 1957 and No. 10 – 2883 of 1962.) Bob Dignam and Peter Sant are seen at work. The works contained an overhead crane as well as the lifting jacks. (Gordon Nutt)

Jack Reynolds who joined Round Oak in 1955 as diesel locomotive engineer. (Jack Reynolds Collection)

The Wagon Repair Department was a busy part of The Wallows complex. Originally the department had built and maintained wooden wagons, but later many more wagons were built of steel or had steel components. In this 1964 photograph we see Eric Hadington and Keith Johnson welding cradles which will be bolted on to the frames of hot ingot transfer wagons. (The cradles were necessary to prevent the ingots moving while in transit.) (Round Oak Collection)

In 1978, this wooden-bodied open wagon that had been used on the trains between Baggeridge and Round Oak was handed over to the Birmingham Railway Museum for preservation. On the right we see Jim Fowler, director of marketing at Round Oak, handing the wagon over to Jim Kent of the museum. The white Pensnett Railway lettering on the red oxide livery of the wagon was applied by David Faithful. (Round Oak Collection)

Bill Fletcher, of the Wagon Repair Workshops, is seen applying red oxide paint to a Pensnett Railway wooden-bodied open wagon in 1964. (Round Oak Collection)

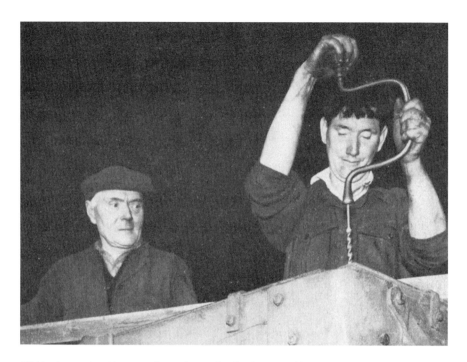

Bill Hughes assists Moses Farley as he applies his brace and bit to the task of wagon repairs at The Wallows in 1964. (Round Oak Collection)

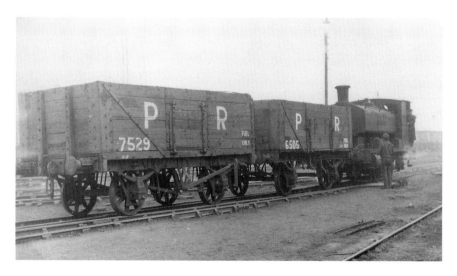

Lady Morvyth (Andrew Barclay 0-4-0ST 2054 of 1938) shunts two wagons at The Wallows after they have received attention in the Wagon Repairs Workshop in about 1960. A huge number of wagons were in use on the Pensnett Railway – some built at The Wallows for specialised use within the works, and a large number of second-hand wooden-bodied open wagons such as these. (Round Oak Collection)

Photographs in the gloom of the running shed are more uncommon but enough daylight pours in from the entrance to illuminate this view of *Jubilee* and her crew in 1963. (Round Oak Collection)

In the 1960s one of the most striking features of the area just north of The Wallows was the lines of withdrawn BR locomotives and wagons awaiting the cutter's torch. The furnaces at Round Oak consumed vast quantities of scrap iron. Here we see *Lady Morvyth* shunting a dead ex-GWR pannier tank locomotive on to the scrap line in 1960. (John Dew)

The scrapping crew move in on ex-GWR 0-6-0PT 5788 on the scrap lines at the back of The Wallows. Wooden-bodied wagons were often set alight to reduce them to their metal components. Locomotives had to be dismantled more slowly. (Michael Hale Collection)

Scrapping locomotives and rolling stock at The Wallows produced some unusual sights at this location. In April 1966, two ex-Great Central Railway class 04 2-8-0 locomotives arrived, having been withdrawn by the Eastern Region of British Railways. They were BR Nos 63570 and 63920. (Viv Morgan)

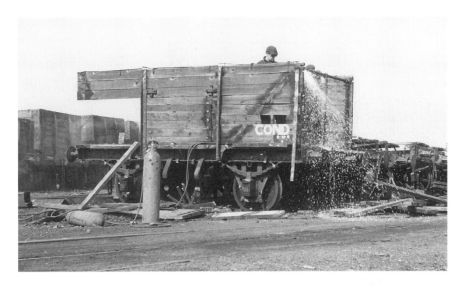

Vast numbers of wagons arrived at The Wallows for scrapping in the early 1960s. They were usually hoisted from the track by a mobile crane and arranged in rows to await the cutter's torch. Sometimes wooden bodies were burned off to make access to the metalwork easier. Meanwhile, some local residents raided the wagons to maintain their own supplies of coal. This picture was taken in 1963. (Viv Morgan)

When steam locomotives were withdrawn from service on the Pensnett Railway in June 1963, they also made their way to the sidings at the back of The Wallows to await scrapping. Nameplates were removed and two engines were retained (*Lady Honor* and *Lady Morvyth*) in case the diesels were confronted with a fuel crisis. Here we see *Billy*, *Lady Patricia* and *Princess Margaret* in 'death row' in 1963. (Viv Morgan)

Three years later *Lady Honor* and *Lady Morvyth* were scrapped. *Lady Morvyth*, seen here on 7 March 1966, was the last to go, and Viv Morgan recorded the fairly rapid demise of the locomotive in a series of photographs. (Viv Morgan)

In happier times *Lady Morvyth* is seen here at Prices' Brickworks Siding in February 1951. It was ambitious of Keith Gale to attempt to record the scene on such a wintry day, but fortunately it provides us with a rare glimpse of a rarely photographed part of the system. Keith himself was fairly dismissive of such pictures and never considered publishing them, partly because they seemed too recent, and partly because no one realised how quickly such scenes would become part of the past. (Keith Gale)

8

Serving the Works at Round Oak

The history of the works at Round Oak is complicated and beyond the scope of this book. The story reflects the Ward family's involvement in industrial matters – a subject that has been described in Trevor Raybould's *The Economic Emergence of the Black Country*. Where they did not directly become involved in mining or iron-making, they did so via lessees and sub-contractors, often making sure they benefitted financially from rents and royalties on final products. For example, in the area under consideration, it seems that Messrs W. & R. Croft leased land on The Level on the fringe of Brierley Hill to build a small iron-making furnace in 1784.

The industrialisation of this area followed the opening of the Dudley and Stourbridge canals, both in 1779. The former was only 2¼ miles long – from just south of Parkhead to the bottom of the Delph Locks but it skirted Brierley Hill by following the contours – i.e. The Level. The 1784 furnace referred to above was built on the south side of the canal and was known as the Old Level Iron Works. In 1788 Messrs Gibbons leased land on which they built a mill and forge, but two years later they took over the site on the southern side of the canal and built The New Level Works, adding furnaces until, in about 1814, they had four producing iron. Thirty years later, in 1844, Messrs Gibbons moved to the Corbyn's Hall Iron Works, and The New Level Works was brought directly under the control of Viscount Ward via his agent, Richard Smith. The latter remodelled the New Level Iron Works from the mid-1840s onwards – a period already identified in previous chapters as the time when the Pensnett Railway emerged.

Everything changed again in the mid-1850s when Richard Smith started building his new 'model' ironworks on the northern side of the canal: the Round Oak Iron Works, which began production in 1857. The new works enjoyed proximity to the canal, the new main line of the Oxford, Worcester and Wolverhampton Railway, the Earl's own growing railway system and even the Earl's own canal with its basin at The Wallows.

By the mid-1890s steel-making had come to Round Oak and this continued through various modernisations of the process until 1983. Throughout the whole period from 1857 to 1982 the works went through endless changes and therefore the railway did likewise – eventually becoming nothing more than an internal railway system almost completely contained within the works. This chapter reveals the distinctive visual quality enjoyed by the Pensnett Railway while performing its 'works system' role.

A glimpse of Round Oak Iron Works in the 1860s shows one of the E.B. Wilson-type locomotives at work on the lines that passed the front of the original buildings. (Keith Gale Collection)

The Pensnett Railway within Round Oak Works provides striking pictures of locomotives and trains in exciting industrial settings. Here we see *Princess Margaret* at work (Andrew Barclay 0-4-0ST 2115 of 1941) in 1963, the last year of steam, propelling a slag wagon. (Viv Morgan Collection)

Lady Edith (Andrew Barclay 0-4-0ST 2117 of 1941). (Peter Shoesmith)

An unidentified Andrew Barclay 0-4-0ST poses in the Round Oak landscape on 2 May 1959. The chimneys of the open-hearth shop provide an iconic setting alongside all the other details: metal 'rubbish wagons' in the background, wooden-bodied coal wagons in Pensnett Railway livery in the foreground, a typical Earl of Dudley water tank etc. (Peter Shoesmith)

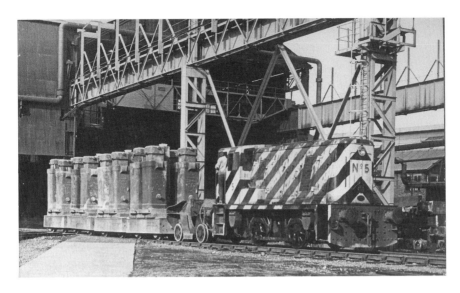

Yorkshire Engine 0-4-0 diesel electric locomotive propels four ingot cars, separated from its train by a 'beetle' which provided safe riding for the shunter and kept the locomotive away from the hot ingots. (Viv Morgan Collection)

Yorkshire Engine Co. diesel electric locomotive No. 10 (2883 of 1962). Metal wagons were used for transporting scrap from the stockpiles of such material to the furnaces as seen in this picture taken within weeks of the works' closure. (Keith Hodgkins)

One aspect of life at Round Oak centred around the crossings in Level Street. Here we see one of the Andrew Barclay 0-4-0STs plus a slag-bowl wagon on the Level Street Crossing on 2 May 1959. Beyond the train some people are leaning against the parapet of the canal bridge. There is still a canal bridge at this location to help us imagine the site of the crossing. (Peter Shoesmith)

Yorkshire Engine 0-4-0 diesel electric locomotive No. 10 seen from the Level Street Crossing on 20 February 1964. This was the 'lower' crossing, of 1959 vintage. Note the chimney of the Level Street Mill. (Viv Morgan)

Yorkshire Engine 0-4-0 diesel electric locomotive No. 2 takes a slag-bowl wagon out to the back of the works in its final days of operation and tips the slag into an area that was later to be turned into a home for the Merry Hill shopping complex. (Keith Hodgkins)

As well as the road crossings in Level Street, another well-known feature of the Pensnett Railway in the works' area was the level crossing with the GWR West Midlands line. Here we see *Duchess of Gloucester* (Andrew Barclay 0-6-0ST 2110 of 1941) on the crossing in 1956. (Round Oak Collection)

The original route of the level crossing had to be realigned in the 1970s to accommodate a major modernisation of the works. In the process, the crossing was going to move a few yards towards Dudley. (Round Oak Collection)

The level crossing at Round Oak in its 'new' position in about 1974. (Round Oak Collection)

Relaying track at Round Oak in the 1975 summer shutdown. In the background is the No. 2 Melting Shop. In the foreground, track is being relaid to the Level Street Crossing. (Round Oak Collection)

Yorkshire Engine Co. diesel electric 0-4-0 locomotive No. 1 (2593 of 1955) stands just in front of a new crossing installed in yet another modernisation of the Round Oak Steel Works, as late as 1980, looking towards the stripping and soaking pit bays. (Gordon Nutt)

Yorkshire Engine Co. diesel electric 0-4-0 locomotive No. 3 (2662 of 1957) undertaking the journey between The Wallows and Round Oak Steel Works on 21 September 1980. Even when the Pensnett Railway was reduced to simply being a 'works system', engines still had to leave the works to reach their stable. (Gordon Nutt)

Andrew Barclay 0-6-0ST *Prince of Wales* stands between The Wallows and The Terrace in 1954, in front of new steel mineral wagons. (Roger Carpenter Collection)

9

Men at Work

The Pensnett Railway employed a large number of people. Once the system was 'unified' in 1865, the number of people working on the railway seemed to settle at between 150 and 160 men. Sometimes a surviving record gives a very precise number. For example, T.M. Hoskison came across a Christmas Beef List of 1876 which identified 137 men plus 15 boys, producing a total of 152, plus some unidentified managers and clerks. After the closure of the Castle Mill Works, the number of specialised craftsmen employed at The Wallows grew considerably, although within a decade or two the line was beginning to shrink.

As at Round Oak Steel Works, there were many cases of whole families working on the Pensnett Railway in the sense that sons followed fathers who followed their fathers. This was also true at a management level, and two families often mentioned are the Mantle and the Mace families.

The Mantles were a very important Woodside family in the second half of the nineteenth century. Joshua Parkes Mantle lived in a large house in Pensnett Road, Holly Hall, virtually opposite the top of Low Town. He was born in 1818, and from the age of about 30 onwards worked for the Earl of Dudley until his death in 1899. His father, John Mantle, had been a malster, associated with The Saracens Head in Dudley, and The Stewponey, Kinver. (John's sister was Julia Hanson, the Dudley brewer.)

Joshua Parkes Mantle had been employed in the cutting of the Dudley railway tunnel in the mid-1840s, and then became a surface manager at the Earl of Dudley's collieries. (He is said to have been involved in the cutting of Ashwood Basin, but he would have been eleven when that first came into use when the Earl's railway opened, so is more likely to have been involved in later improvements to it.) Eventually, he became transport manager of the Earl's railway. Interestingly, he is described as 'colliery agent' in the 1881 census, but then railway manager in the 1891 one.

Joshua married Ann and they had about ten children, some of who became associated with mining, others were publicans and brewers, and Joshua Mantle the younger became associated with Hollies Farm, Pensnett. Joshua Mantle the

Joshua Parkes Mantle (1818–99). (Round Oak Collection)

Leonard Mace (1890–1960). (Round Oak Collection)

elder was a devout Anglican and became a church warden at St Augustine's, Holly Hall. He was also an ardent Conservative but never succeeded in being elected to Dudley Council. He was a popular figure with the railwaymen on the Pensnett Railway and six of them carried his coffin at his funeral.

Joshua Parkes Mantle's son, Reuben (born 1849), also worked for the Earl of Dudley for some sixty years – probably ten years more than his father. He was particularly associated with the Castle Mill Works. He was one of the Mantles who had lived at Bridge House that stood at the point where the Earl's railway passed under Pensnett Road and entered the Old Park. The site of the house, and Mantle's Bridge, is now occupied by a busy road island close to Russells Hall Hospital.

Once he took charge of the Castle Mill Works, Reuben lived close to the works, but continued strong connections with Holly Hall and Pensnett. He was a Dudley councillor from 1903 until his death in April 1925.

Charles Mace (1821–1901) came from Yorkshire to drive a contractor's locomotive on the building of the Oxford, Worcester and Wolverhampton Railway in the 1840s, but seems to have soon transferred to the Pensnett Railway. His appointment in 1846 is just in that period when the railway was being established. Unfortunately we do not know what locomotives he would have first driven, as nothing is known about the locomotive stock of the Pensnett Railway until the arrival of *Alma* in 1855.

Charles Mace stayed on the Pensnett Railway for the rest of his working life and was followed by his son, William Mace. William Mace (1862–1939) left school at the age of 12 and started work in one of the Earl of Dudley's pits. He transferred to the Pensnett Railway as soon as he could and eventually became a driver – a job he did until the age of 70.

In turn, William was followed by his son, Leonard (1890–1960). He left school at 14 and became a messenger boy on the Pensnett Railway in 1903. He was promoted to the role of shunter, then joined the footplate as a fireman and then became a driver. From 1926 until 1956 he was traffic inspector on the Baggeridge Section.

When steam traction ceased in 1963 there seemed to be a feeling that history was being made and pictures were taken 'for the record'. For example, Douglas Heath took pictures like this one of a driver on the footplate of *Billy* (Andrew Barclay 1881 of 1925) within the works. However the driver was not identified by name – perhaps on the assumption that everyone in the Round Oak 'family' knew it. One of the frustrations fifty years later is the difficulty of identifying the people who worked on the Pensnett Railway. (Round Oak Collection)

Everyone posed for the camera in this picture of *Victory* but no one recorded their names. *Victory* started out as an 0-4-0 tender locomotive (Manning Wardle 94 of 1863) and was later rebuilt in this form as an 0-4-2ST at the Castle Mill Works. (Peter George Collection)

When Michael Hale took this picture of *Lady Patricia* at The Wallows in 1954, he took the trouble to record the identities of the crew: J. Jackson and D. Curtis. In 1983, Michael Hale was able to buy *Lady Patricia*'s nameplate. (Michael Hale)

The end of steam at The Wallows, June 1963. Front left to right: Tom Batham (fitter), Paddy, Bill Holden (yard foreman), Stan Staves (shed foreman); up by the smokebox: Ted Hamilton (boilersmith); by the side of the engine: Charlie Tomkins and Les Willis (fitters); on the footplate: Alan Manton. (Jack Reynolds Collection)

Bill Holden at his desk in his role as assistant wagon repairs foreman (assistant to Stan Staves) in 1964. About forty wagons passed through the works each week and Bill had to keep an eye on the progress of every one of them. (Round Oak Collection)

Bill Holden poses for a picture by one of the Pensnett Railway wagons. He left school at the age of 14 in 1924 and joined the railway as an apprentice wagon repairer. He retired at the age of 68, in 1978, as assistant wagon repairs foreman. He lived to celebrate his 100th birthday and put the secret of living a long life down to his work on the railway. (Round Oak Collection)

Harold Downing (boiler cleaner) and Ted Hamilton (boilersmith) inspect *Princess Margaret* (Andrew Barclay 0-4-0ST 2115 of 1941) outside the locomotive repair shed at The Wallows in 1960. *Princess Margaret* was the last locomotive in steam at Round Oak. (Viv Morgan Collection)

Another picture taken, probably by Douglas Heath, to record the end of steam in June 1963. Standing left to right: unknown shunter, Joe Cooper (shunter), Ernie Hillman, Sidney Didlock (shunter) and Taffy Roberts (controller). On the footplate: Ron Winfield and Maty Alport. (Jack Reynolds Collection)

Opposite top: *Jubilee* (Andrew Barclay 0-6-0ST 2012 of 1935) looks new in this picture, suggesting that the employee was posed alongside the locomotive when the newcomer arrived or when it was cleaned to work the trains to the fetes at Himley. (Dudley Archives)

Opposite bottom: George Williamson was a platelayer who had worked on most branches of the Pensnett Railway in a forty-five-year career. After eight years at Askew Bridge he decided to retire in September 1966 when the coal trains ceased running to Round Oak. He died on 29 July 1975 at the age of 74. (Round Oak Collection)

On 26 September 1966, Douglas Heath went out to record the passage of the last coal train from Askew Bridge to Round Oak and took this picture before the final journey began behind diesel locomotive No. 10. Left to right: D. Davies (shunter), M. Westbury (senior shunter), R. Hickman (Wallows traffic foreman), George Chatham, L. Smith (driver), J. Lloyd (traffic foreman). (Douglas Heath)

In May 1962, Josiah Hickman decided that the approaching end of steam on the Pensnett Railway would be a good time to retire from his post as traffic manager. Here he is seen standing in front of the Yorkshire Engine Co. diesel electric 0-4-0 No. 4 (2774 of 1959) and *Princess Elizabeth* (Andrew Barclay 0-4-0ST 2016 of 1935). (Round Oak Collection)

The transition from steam to diesel in June 1963 was also marked by the retirement of the old mobile crane – which had already been dieselised anyway! It was usually driven by Bill Prosser who had worked at Round Oak since starting in the Cogging Mill in 1924. Bill had also played cricket for Round Oak for thirty years. (Round Oak Collection)

Sam Holloway takes a last look at the retired steam locomotives in July 1964, at the time of his own retirement. Sam started work at Round Oak in 1913 in the Old Level Mill. When that mill closed in 1946 he transferred to the railway and became a platelayer and later joined the locomotive maintenance department. (Round Oak Collection)

Bill Wilmott (railway services engineer) hands a wristwatch to Ted Davies to mark the latter's retirement in January 1974. Ted had worked as a diesel repairs fitter for seven years, and is seen here with other maintenance staff. (Round Oak Collection)

Viceroy (Andrew Barclay 0-4-0ST, 954 of 1903) is the subject of a good locomotive portrait with an intriguing line-up of unidentified staff. The driver is obviously on the footplate, and his fireman may be standing on the right of the picture, with the shunter in the centre, but the figure on the left of the picture is a mystery. (Dudley Archives)

J. Walker (on the right) is identified as this crossing keeper at Stallings Lane in 1949. These beehive-shaped crossing keeper's huts were a feature of the Pensnett Railway. (Viv Morgan)

10

Locomotives and Rolling Stock

The Earl of Dudley's railway system used steam locomotives for over 100 years – from 1829 to 1963 – and continued to use its own fleet of diesel electric locomotives until Round Oak Steel Works closed in 1982. The railway also eventually ran a huge fleet of wagons, and some specialised items of rolling stock. Although *Agenoria* became the well-known motive power on the Kingswinford Railway from 1829 onwards, and survives today in the National Railway Museum at York, we know nothing about the first locomotives that ran from the mid-1840s onwards on the Pensnett Railway. All we know is that *Alma* arrived in 1855, and that began a policy of ordering similar locomotives – firstly from E.B. Wilson of the Railway Foundry in Leeds, and then from his successor: Messrs Manning Wardle. (Some of these locomotives were assembled at Castle Mill Works from parts supplied by Manning Wardle.)

Later there was some experimentation with locomotives from other manufacturers – such as Peckett, the locomotive builders based in Bristol – but from the mid-1920s onwards the builder of choice eventually became Andrew Barclay of Kilmarnock. The 0-4-0ST prevailed but 0-6-0STs were purchased when engines of greater power were needed and for work on the railway's main line to Baggeridge Colliery. Locomotives arrived in a smart green livery, attractively lined etc., by the manufacturers, but went on to suffer quite a hard life on the Pensnett Railway. Towards the end of steam, in the post-Second World War era, the engines were worked ruthlessly, and there was less pride in maintaining their appearance. By the end of the 1950s, crews couldn't wait to see traffic handled by new, cleaner and more powerful diesel electric locomotives.

Ednam was supplied to the Pensnett Railway as late as 1872 – arriving as a kit of parts at the Castle Mills Works from Manning Wardle – still very much in the E.B. Wilson style. The locomotive was eventually scrapped in 1926. (Viv Morgan Collection)

Queen was an 0-6-0 side tank supplied by Manning Wardle (227) in 1867, and worked until 1896 on the Shut End Railway, i.e. the system which served the ironworks and collieries owned by John Bradley & Co. The decline of the Shut End Works and the extinguishing of their furnaces in the mid-1890s probably accounts for the locomotive's absorption by the Pensnett Railway. Although an 0-6-0 side tank, *Queen* displays many of the features of the early Manning Wardle locomotives, particularly the fluted dome and basic windshield 'weather protection' for the crew. (Keith Gale Collection)

The first *Lady Edith* was this Peckett 0-4-0ST (488 of 1890) It was rebuilt at Castle Mill Works in 1920 and survived until 1934 – the name reappearing on an Andrew Barclay 0-6-0ST in 1941. In the background we can see a more modern Peckett, *Bristol* (1389 of 1915), also scrapped in 1934. (Keith Gale Collection)

This picture of Round Oak illustrates the way in which vintage locomotives could be rebuilt at the Castle Mill Works and be given a new lease of life. The locomotive probably began life as a Manning Wardle 0-4-0 tender engine (176 of 1865). It was rebuilt in this form in 1907, as an 0-4-2ST, and was scrapped in the mid-1920s. It was one of two 0-4-2STs to be used by the Pensnett Railway, the other being *Victory.* (Viv Morgan Collection)

This Avonside 0-4-0ST (1802 of 1918) was the 'exception to the rule' on a railway system that was eventually dominated by Andrew Barclay locomotives. It was scrapped in 1949. (Viv Morgan Collection)

Princess Margaret, an Andrew Barclay 0-4-0ST (2115 of 1941), was one of the engines to arrive at Round Oak to cope with heavy wartime traffic. The 'front end' is typical of the engines used from that time onwards within the Round Oak Steel Works, with the distinctive handrail and step on which the shunter could travel, and the extra buffer beam below the standard buffers. (Michael Hale Collection)

The first *Lady Morvyth* was a Peckett 0-6-0ST (1568 of 1921) and was one of a pair of engines – the other being *Lady Rosemary* (1577 of 1921) seen on page 35. These were larger engines bought to work on the main line and with a view to working the Barrow Hill Incline unassisted. This locomotive was scrapped in 1938. (Viv Morgan Collection)

The Andrew Barclay 0-4-0STs going about their work were ideal subjects for photography, and any book about the Pensnett Railway soon fills up with them. On 19 April 1952, *Winston* (Andrew Barclay 0-4-0ST 2116 of 1942) is seen here at The Wallows with a train of 'rubbish wagons'. (Tim Shuttleworth)

A portrait of *Lady Honor* (Andrew Barclay 2031 of 1937) survived until the end of steam in 1963 but was not immediately scrapped like most of her sisters. *Lady Honor* and *Lady Morvyth* were put aside just in case there were needed on 'stand-by' duties. They were finally scrapped in March 1966, allegedly in a fit of pique! The locomotives on the Pensnett Railway were often named after the children of William Ward, 2nd Earl of Dudley. (Jack Reynolds Collection)

Prince of Wales (Andrew Barclay 2002 of 1934) was one of the 0-6-0STs bought for use on the main line, principally to bring coal to Round Oak from Baggeridge Colliery. In doing this job they managed to remain cleaner and in better condition than some of the locomotives that worked hard and unceasingly in the steelworks. This locomotive was scrapped in 1962 but nameplates were removed and carefully stored. In about 1982, in the final days of the steelworks, many if not all of the nameplates were offered for sale and are now in the collections of enthusiasts. (Jack Reynolds Collection)

Two Andrew Barclay 0-6-0STs stand in the sunshine at The Wallows at the beginning of the 1960s with little sense that their lives are nearly over. (John Dew)

The steam locomotives were withdrawn in 1963 and all but two were unceremoniously taken to the sidings beyond The Wallows and were cut up for scrap. As they awaited the cutter's torch they were stripped of nameplates and makers' plates and seemed not only forlorn but also anonymous. (Michael Hale)

Although *Lady Honor* and *Lady Morvyth* were not scrapped immediately, they too were eventually cut up in March 1966. This took a number of people by surprise and one legend surrounding this was that the nameplate of *Lady Morvyth* was cut in two. (Viv Morgan Collection)

The Yorkshire Engine Company 0-4-0 diesel electric locomotives began to appear at Round Oak in 1955. While the steam locomotives had generally been identified by name, the diesels remained as numbers. Ten were delivered between 1955 and 1962. No. 11 was added in 1969, having been purchased second-hand. Here we see No. 5 running cab-first near Level Street on 10 January 1964. (Viv Morgan)

No. 0 was built by Robert Stephenson & Hawthorn in 1940 for the Air Ministry. It came to the Pensnett Railway in 1953 but saw little use. It was scrapped at Cashmore's yard in 1960. (Michael Hale)

The Pensnett Railway owned a large fleet of wagons, but obviously no carriages. The wooden-bodied open wagons are seen in many of the pictures in this book. Open wagons were used for carrying coal, and within the works were used for carrying scrap metal. (Viv Morgan)

Of particular interest were the small number of wagons used for 'departmental' purposes. The platelayers used the wagons seen here, and several vans. Van No. 3 was an ex-GWR van built in 1915, still in use on the Pensnett Railway when photographed in 1963. No. 2 was a similar van built in 1924. (Viv Morgan)

Van No. 4 was a guard's van which saw occasional use on the Himley fete trains. (Keith Gale)

Bill Prosser's mobile crane (see page 115). This was originally steam powered, but by the time it was withdrawn in 1963 it had had a diesel engine fitted. (Round Oak Collection)

A row of tipping slag-bowl wagons, photographed in the works in 1963, shows that there were two sizes of such vehicles. (Viv Morgan)

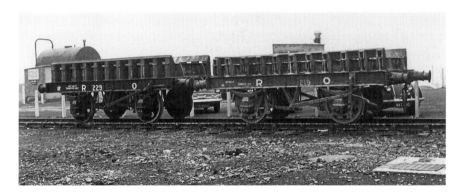

Two billet wagons, numbered 229 and 219, looking rather 'new' when photographed on 27 November 1963. (Viv Morgan)

11

Carrying Passengers

Although the Kingswinford Railway had carried guests when it opened on 2 June 1829, the railways described in this book did not set out to be passenger-carrying lines. No doubt there were 'unofficial passengers' carried now and again, and the occasional official party of visitors, but the lines had no facilities for dealing with passenger traffic. In the summer of 1912, a meeting of the Iron & Steel Institute was held in a marquee at Round Oak Steel Works. Guests were invited to travel by train to Baggeridge Colliery and occupied benches installed in cleaned-out coal wagons lined with fresh straw. Such occasions were very rare, and the real story of 'passenger traffic' on the Pensnett Railway concerns only the special trains provided from 1928 until 1937 to take employees and their families from Round Oak (The Wallows) to Himley for the annual fetes held in the grounds of Himley Hall.

These services were first introduced in August 1928. Eight open wagons installed with benches were provided for the 3-mile journey. (The wagons carried the letters 'E' and 'D' in the livery of the time.) Pensnett Railway staff travelled in each wagon to warn passengers of the dangers of passing through bridges with limited clearances, particularly the bridge at the top of the Barrow Hill Incline. The locomotive *Jeremy* was put in charge of the trains and the railway's guard's van was also attached. It is assumed the trains were 'pulled' from The Wallows to Himley and 'pushed' on the return journey. Trains ran on Thursday, Friday and Saturday, although the fete ran for five days.

The use of open wagons was not repeated and thereafter four-wheel coaches were hired from the Great Western Railway. They were apparently coaches used in workmen's trains in the South Wales coalfield and were brought up to Round Oak especially for the occasion. The Pensnett Railway staff fitted metal bars across the windows of the coaches just in case anyone was tempted to lean out of the window while approaching the narrow bridges. Trains seemed to have consisted of four coaches, one of which was a brake-third. Locomotives used in subsequent years included *Peter* and *Jubilee*. Whichever locomotive was used for these trains, it was always given a thorough cleaning before the occasion.

Tickets had to be obtained from the Pensnett Railway office and were issued on production of an official invitation handed to employees on a departmental basis. Family members were welcome but 'gatecrashers' were discouraged. However, some people obtained tickets for a number of trips and others seemed to have obtained tickets for neighbours and friends. Very temporary platforms were provided at The Wallows and at High Arcal – the point on the Baggeridge line nearest to Himley Hall.

The tickets issued for journeys to and from the fetes at Himley were 'proper' railway company tickets produced by the Bell Punch Company. (Round Oak Collection)

This picture conveys the excitement of travel on the Pensnett Railway for those visiting the Earl of Dudley's fete at Himley Park in 1928. The wagons look freshly painted, even with white tyres to the wheels. Everyone is smartly dressed and the Pensnett Railway manager, Frank Blackburn, is seen hanging onto brake van No. 4 while smoking his pipe. The picture is thought to have been taken at The Wallows. (Round Oak Collection)

Peter and a train of GWR four-wheel coaches is photographed at The Wallows in 1932. Note the bars on the windows. (Keith Gale Collection)

Peter (Andrew Barclay 0-6-0ST, 1965 of 1929) is about to leave The Wallows in 1932 with a train for Himley Park. It is just possible to glimpse one of the GWR coaches used on these trains. (Round Oak Collection)

Some idea of the nature of the 'temporary platform' used at The Wallows can be gained from this picture. (Round Oak Collection)

This picture suggests that no platform was provided at Himley, but other photographs show a platform similar to the one illustrated on this page at The Wallows. (Round Oak Collection)

This photograph was captioned 'En-route for Himley Park Fete' but the surroundings suggest the train is actually at the Himley Park end of its trip. (Round Oak Collection)

The pictures in this montage, taken during the 1928 Himley Park fete, were later published in *The Acorn* of spring 1957. Looking at the bottom left-hand picture, it seems that the usual shunter becomes a uniformed 'guard' for the occasion – probably also one of the few occasions when the Pensnett Railway's brake van was used. (Round Oak Collection)

12

Other Railways at Pensnett

Although it is convenient and sensible to call the Earl of Dudley's railway system The Pensnett Railway, the name does cause some confusion. In this book we have used the term 'Pensnett Railway' to describe the unified system created in 1865 when the Earl's railways radiating from Round Oak were linked to the original 1829 line from Shut End to Ashwood Basin that we have called 'the Kingswinford Railway'. There are two other contenders when it comes to looking at the railways of Pensnett:

This photograph was taken from the overbridge carrying the Dudley–Kingswinford road in about 1963, looking straight into the area once known as Shut End. An ex-GWR 0-6-0 pannier tank shunts the sidings on the right, and the lines still stretch northwards to Baggeridge Junction and to Wombourn. The sidings on the left were once known as John Bradley's sidings, then Pitt's sidings, and are therefore a remnant of the Shut End Railway. This picture brings together the lines described in this chapter: the GWR Kingswinford Branch, and the more obscure Shut End Railway. What is more, the original line of the Kingswinford Railway of 1829 crossed this scene from left to right and curved out of the right-hand side of the picture to reach the Earl of Dudley's pits at Corbyn's Hall. (Viv Morgan)

BR Class 45 locomotive 45045 shunts at Pensnett in 1983 on what has become the northern terminus of the Kingswinford Branch (universally known simply as the Pensnett Branch by this time). The LCP coal concentration depot now dominates the scene, with the company's 0-4-0 shunter *Peter* on the left, and the wagon-hauling cable engine house seen in the background. In the last twenty years the scene has been transformed yet again and all signs of the railways are disappearing. (Viv Morgan)

1. The branch of what became the GWR, which terminated at Askew Bridge and Oak Farm until being extended in the twentieth century to Wombourn and on to Wolverhampton.

2. The railway which served the Shut End collieries and ironworks and which survived to serve the Pensnett Trading Estate.

Let us call the former the Kingswinford Branch, and the latter can be called the Shut End Railway.

The Kingswinford Branch

The Kingswinford Branch goes back to the days of the Oxford, Worcester and Wolverhampton Railway (the OWWR, or 'Old Worse and Worse'). The OWWR's main line approached the Black Country via Stourbridge Junction, and crossed the Stour Valley on an impressive viaduct at Stambermill. From there it climbed up to Brierley Hill, and continued to climb all the way to Dudley and then on to Wolverhampton. It opened as far as Dudley in 1852 and to Wolverhampton in 1854. In doing so it traversed the south-western corner of the Black Country on which we have focussed, and crossed the Earl of Dudley's railway at Round Oak.

In 1858, the OWWR opened a branch from Kingswinford Junction – just north of Brettell Lane – to Bromley Basin at the junction of the Stourbridge Canal and the Stourbridge Extension Canal. A couple of years later the branch was pushed northwards into the Shut End area and eventually terminated close to where the line forked – one line terminating close to the Oak Farm Ironworks, the other terminating at Askew Bridge. The latter provided a point at which it could be later connected to the Earl of Dudley's Pensnett Railway. The OWWR was absorbed into the West Midland Railway and then the Great Western Railway – hence we talk of the Kingswinford Branch of the GWR.

The Kingswinford Branch, the Stourbridge Extension Canal, and the Earl of Dudley's Pensnett Railway, therefore, all played their part in opening up the collieries, ironworks and brickworks of the area west of Pensnett village which is often called Shut End. Like all Black Country place names this can seem to be very 'vague' and ill-defined, the next minute it seems very particular. If someone today asks 'Where is Shut End?', the answer could be that it is the area between the villages of Pensnett and Kingswinford which is now largely covered by the Pensnett Trading Estate.

In the twentieth century, the GWR's freight-only Kingswinford Branch became part of a wider scheme in which the company would link Wolverhampton with Bridgnorth and provide access to the East Shropshire Coalfield. In the end, all this materialised in a line which doubled and extended the Kingswinford Branch and took it out through Himley and Woodbourne and on to Wolverhampton. All this was being planned at the same time that the GWR was participating in building the line from Askew Bridge up to Baggeridge Colliery – to be worked by the Pensnett Railway. It was relevant to the interests of the GWR in that coal would also be able to travel over their railway via a point which was to be called Baggeridge Junction, close to the old Oak Farm terminus of the Kingswinford Branch. All this can seem very complicated but can be clarified by studying maps or consulting *The Railway to Wombourn* (Ned Williams, Uralia Press, 1986).

The Wombourn extension of the Kingswinford Branch opened in 1925 for both freight and passengers. The latter provision resulted in halts being opened at Gornal and Pensnett in the area with which we are concerned, but these were only used until passenger services ceased in 1932. The Wombourn line closed to remaining freight traffic in 1965 which almost brought us back to where we began. After 1965, we were left with a line from Kingswinford to Pensnett – much as we had 100 years earlier.

The Kingswinford Branch continued to enjoy a complicated history. The line between Pensnett and Baggeridge Junction closed in April 1968, but Pensnett continued to be a point where the main-line railway system met the remaining part of the Shut End Railway – the other railway that has a claim in serving this area.

The Shut End Railway

Almost as soon as the original Kingswinford Railway of 1829 had opened between Ashford Basin and Shut End, James Foster began building an integrated ironworks at Shut End. The furnaces at Shut End were in production by 1831. A 'branch' of the Kingswinford Railway climbed another incline to serve the new furnaces, and met the KR close to the point where an engine shed had been built to house *Agenoria* – just north of St Mary's Church, Kingswinford. James Foster, of course, owned *Agenoria* and the relationship between the KR and Foster was subject to complicated agreements.

In 1885, William Orme Foster decided not to renew existing agreements and from then on the Ashwood Branch was exclusively worked by the Pensnett Railway (with which it had been physically joined since 1865) and the railways within the Shut End Works were operated separately in the name of John Bradley & Co. These lines became what we shall call the Shut End Railway.

The Shut End Railway had its own locomotives in the shape of *Prince of Wales* (Manning Wardle 166 of 1865), *Queen* (Manning Wardle 227 of 1867) and the *Princess of Wales* (Manning Wardle 708 of 1879). These were able to work a network of lines at Shut End that connected the ironworks to surrounding pits, coke ovens, and brickworks, and handed traffic to and from the Pensnett Railway at the 'frontier' close to the old engine shed mentioned above. Shut End Railway traffic at Ashwood seemed to enjoy the use of separate sidings, but who was employed by whom to do what remains quite a mystery, as the George family, based at Ashwood, seem to have been employed both by the Earl of Dudley and the Shut End Railway.

The Shut End Iron Works declined as a result of a recession in the iron trades in the 1880s and then the rise of 'steel'. The furnaces were blown out in the 1890s but some of the pits, in a Shut End 'series', seem to have continued to be worked. In 1913, the remaining business was bought by H.S. Pitt & Co. The new owners seem to have acquired *Princess of Wales* and *Coneygre* – an ex-Pensnett Railway engine that came to Shut End in 1896. (*Queen* had already transferred to the Pensnett Railway.)

H.S. Pitt & Co. became Guy Pitt & Co. in 1925, by which time there were three pits left in operation, and *Princess of Wales* had been scrapped but had been 'replaced' with *David* – a Manning Wardle locomotive (774 of 1881) which had been used by the contractor who had built the railway to Wombourn. Guy Pitt

& Co. later reopened the Standhills Colliery which they could only reach by rail via the GWR Kingswinford Branch through Pensnett. A study of maps suggests that originally the line to Standhills had run alongside the Kingswinford Branch, but was possibly swallowed up by the main-line company in their upgrading of the Kingswinford Branch. Whatever the explanation, we have photographic evidence of a Shut End Railway engine (*Peter*) passing through Pensnett, even though such practices were supposed to have ceased in 1947 with the nationalisation of the coal industry. The study of maps in this area only confirms how complicated the Shut End network was and how it constantly changed.

Most of the Shut End collieries were worked out and abandoned by the end of the 1930s, but then the Second World War came along and activity returned to Shut End. Furnace waste and old coal banks could now provide hard core on which to build airfield runways. By the end of the war there was so much activity in the Shut End area that Guy Pitt & Co. bought two new (second-hand) locomotives: *Winston Churchill* (Manning Wardle 2025 of 1923) and *Peter* (Andrew Barclay 782 of 1896). Both arrived in 1946.

The company prospered as coal factors, and developed a post-war plan to clean up the Shut End site and gradually turn it into what we now know as a trading estate. Because the Shut End Railway network survived, it was first suggested that this could provide rail access to the estate from the Kingswinford Branch (from 1948 onwards part of the Western Region of British Railways). Progress on the creation of the trading estate was slow, and in the course of the progress, Guy Pitt & Co. ceased to exist, and, from 1960 onwards, the estate and railway were administered by Messrs Lunt, Comley & Pitt (LCP).

Although this photograph only survives in a poor-quality image, it is reproduced here as pictures of the Shut End Railway are rare. Here we see *Princess of Wales* with a shunter's truck and wagon painted in an 'H.S. Pitt' livery. (Peter George Collection)

By the 1960s it was obvious that rail access to the estate was going to be less important to potential tenants than at first thought. However, for a short time, tracks encircled the estate just as they had once encircled the old ironworks. The Shut End Railway enjoyed a swan song in which *Winston Churchill* delivered car parts packed in containers to a tenant on the estate. Meanwhile, LCP redeveloped the point where they connected with the Kingswinford Branch, and in 1964 they opened a coal concentration depot on that site. This was worked by diesel shunters they had bought for the purpose (*Peter* and *Sam*).

All this activity at Shut End provided another forty years' transport history for the site. In this time, LCP moved further into the estates and property world to become London & Cambridge Properties. At Shut End, just north of the site of Pensnett Halt, the remaining part of the railway system saw lots of changes in traffic, ranging from the delivery of pig iron to the delivery of mineral water.

Winston Churchill was last steamed in 1968 and two years later was transferred to a corner-site at the Black Country Museum. It then returned for a time to stand on a plinth in the Pensnett Trading Estate and in 2011 found itself back at the museum. It stands outside the Black Country Living Museum to bring to everyone's attention the importance of industrial railways, but many people feels its ancestry is confusing – partly because the relationships between the railway providers in the Shut End/Pensnett area is complicated, as seen by this chapter.

Shut End Railway locomotive *Princess of Wales*. (Manning Wardle 0-6-0ST 708 of 1879 – not to be confused with the Pensnett Railway's *Prince of Wales*.) This locomotive seems to have come directly to the Shut End system in 1879 as the property of John Bradley & Co., passing to H.S. Pitt & Co. in 1913. (Peter George Collection)

Peter (Andrew Barclay 782 of 1896) at Shut End. Ralph Russell was able to take rather affectionate photographs of industrial locomotives at work, usually with the crew posing for the camera and something of the railways' setting, even if only a brickyard chimney. (Ralph Russell)

Ralph Russell spent a leisurely day at Pensnett on 15 August 1946 and took this excellent portrait of *Winston Churchill* (Manning Wardle 2025 of 1923). The engine had an interesting history, having once worked for Cadbury's, first at Bourneville and then at Worcester. Today (2013) the locomotive stands outside the entrance to the Black Country Museum, having spent many years on a plinth in the Pensnett Trading Estate. (Ralph Russell)

David (Manning Wardle 774 of 1881) at Shut End on 5 April 1946. The engine was bought by H.S. Pitt & Co. from Perry & Co., Woodbourne line contractors, in 1919. (Ralph Russell)

Winston Churchill brings a train of container wagons onto the Pensnett Trading Estate in about 1960. Note the Nissen hut-style building in the background – one of many that once occupied this area. (Viv Morgan)

Winston Churchill was housed in the Shut End Railway's little engine shed. (Viv Morgan)

Peter survived long enough to work some of the trains of container wagons that came onto the Pensnett Trading Estate in the early 1960s. It came to Shut End about 1923 from Kinlet Colliery in Shropshire, and after a period of 'abandonment' at Shut End, it was rescued in 1969 and taken to the Ironbridge Gorge Museum at Blists Hill. (Eric Rogers)

Peter makes its way past Pensnett South signal box on the GWR Kingswinford Branch in about 1946, to gain access to the 'detached' part of the Shut End Railway that went to Standhills Colliery. The colliery was nationalised in 1947 but did not remain open for long. The former down line was designated for Pitt's use after 1932. (Ray Williams)

This picture of *Peter* passing through the site of Pensnett Halt in the late 1940s was taken by signalman Plimley while he was on relief duty at Pensnett South Signal Box. It seems to reinforce the view that the Shut End Railway had exclusive use of this track leaving the running lines of the Pensnett Branch to the right, even though when the halt was first provided the main running lines would have been those on the left of the picture. (Plimley Collection)

13

Working the Railway

As we have seen, the Pensnett Railway was quite a complex system, and one that was always changing. It follows that the way in which the system was worked changed over the years.

From 1829 until the mid-1860s the system was in fact two separate railways – the original Kingswinford Railway from Shut End to Ashwood Basin, and the separate system that grew up with Round Oak at its centre. Once the two railways were joined they became a unified system, however the line to Ashwood was still worked by James Foster's company, owners of *Agenoria* and the inclines and the stationary steam engines that worked them, although the one at Shut End – sometimes known as Foster's Incline – was out of use by then. Agreements were renewed in 1885, in which it was clear that the Earl of Dudley's estate now ran the Ashwood Branch, as it became known, and William Orme Foster (James Foster's successor) ran the railway at Shut End.

The Pensnett Railway was part of the Earl of Dudley's estate, the estate being managed on his lordship's behalf by an agent. In turn, the railway was administered by a manager. Joshua Parkes Mantle has already been identified as someone who took on this role from the mid-1880s until 1899, having previously been in charge of collieries. Beneath the railway's manager were others who looked after 'motive power', or 'traffic', in a growing chain of command. After the closure of the Castle Mill Works it was essential that the Pensnett Railway had a manager in charge of repair and maintenance of locomotives and rolling stock. By the time Messrs Gale and Hoskison were preparing their project on the history of the railway, they had to consult everyone in this structure: Frank Blackburn, railway manager; Josiah Hickman, traffic manager; R.A. Buxton, repair shop manager; and Leonard Mace, then described as traffic foreman. All over the system, people were weighing loads, checking wagons, running the trains and maintaining the track. It must have been a considerable administrative task.

Frank Blackburn, manager of the Pensnett Railway. He joined the Pensnett Railway in April 1926 after service with the London and North Western Railway and the Nigerian Railways. On page 131, Frank Blackburn can be seen in his younger days making sure all is well on the trains to the fetes at Himley Park. (Round Oak Collection)

The offices of the Pensnett Railway at The Wallows, photographed in December 1963. The bay window beneath the gable seen towards the right-hand side of the picture was the location of the Pensnett Railway manager's office. These buildings do not appear on the 1903 OS map of The Wallows area, reinforcing the idea that the development of this site as headquarters of the system was a twentieth-century phenomenon. (Viv Morgan)

Inclines had always been an important feature of the Pensnett Railway and often determined how the line was worked. *Jeremy* is seen here on 30 May 1951, almost at the top of the Barrow Hill Incline, and about to push its loaded train through the 'tunnel' beneath the Dudley–Kingswinford road. Acquiring locomotives with sufficient power to work such inclines unassisted was an important step forward for the Pensnett Railway. (A.W. Croughton)

The Pensnett Railway, as observed by Messrs Hoskison and Gale, in the postwar era was very much a system operated in two parts. This 'division' was described to me by Alan Hallman, a lifelong fan and son-in-law of a Pensnett Railway driver:

Within the staff of the Pensnett Railway there were sub-groups and rivalries. The main division was between those who worked on the internal railway system within Round Oak Steel Works, and those who worked the sprawling branches of the Pensnett Railway. The former felt that they were given the older and smaller engines, capable of traversing the sharp curves within the works, while the Pensnett Railway men on the branches had newer and larger engines! The crews at Round Oak worked the three shifts while the men on the Pensnett Railway worked in different ways reflecting the traffic they were carrying. As the locomotives came off the shed at The Wallows each morning, they did so in an organised set of timings that reflected all the divisions. Obviously the first were the 'works' locos' which set off as the 6 a.m. shift began. From then on there were departures every quarter or half hour as engines and crews went off to different duties – the eighth such departure being at about 8.30 a.m. as the first long train of 'empties' set out for Baggeridge. Even the locomotives had different routines: the works engines worked nine shifts before going to the Wallows for cleaning, washout and overhaul. Pensnett Railway engines were cleaned after every day's work.

Lady Honor (Andrew Barclay 1998 of 1933) photographed in 1950 at The Wallows. With the smokebox handrail and extra lower buffer beam, she is ready for duty within Round Oak Steel Works. (Keith Gale)

The railway as described by Messrs Hoskison and Gale was already declining in route mileage, although as busy as ever in other respects. By the 1960s these two divisions within the railway's operations still existed, but the day-shift work on the Pensnett Railway's branches had become solely a matter of handling the traffic from Baggeridge Colliery. The coal from Baggeridge to Round Oak, including some for sale at the Terrace Wharf, was brought from the colliery down to Askew Bridge by the National Coal Board locomotive (introduced in 1952). The Pensnett Railway's work simply consisted of working the wagons forward to The Wallows. When this traffic ceased in 1966, the 'division of labour' within the Pensnett Railway ceased to exist and the railway became simply a works' railway.

Vernon Lovatt's Account of 'Working on the Pensnett Railway'

As the twenty-first century proceeds, it is going to become impossible to find anyone who can give us a first-hand account of working on the Pensnett Railway. Luckily, on 29 January 1998, I was able to interview Vernon Lovatt in his home at Kingswinford, and he was able to give a clear account of his work on the railway during the 1930s. He covers some information already covered in other chapters but it was a remarkably complete account of the railway and his part in its administration. I have therefore edited his account in only very minor ways:

I started work at the age of 14 on the Pensnett Railway – at a time when the railway was in full use. I worked in the office that was in The Wallows, close to the engine shed, wagon repair shop, and the engineers' shop at the centre of the system. Beyond these workshops was a breeze hearth. At the end of the each day one chap had to collect ash from the ash pit where the engines' fires had been cleaned out, had to clean the ash and remove the clinker and then take the ash down to the hearth where the breeze was made. This breeze was used in the forges by the blacksmiths, and some of it was sold to Mr Lote, who was contracted to remove some of it for sale elsewhere.

Nearby was the canal wharf at the end of the canal that came up from Parkhead. Loaded wagons discharged coal into the boats who then took their cargo all over the place. Beyond that were some sidings on which Pensnett Railway trains were marshalled. From there, one of the lines of the Pensnett Railway ran across to the Old Park, and when I started work the Number 22, 23 and 24 pits were still working on the Old Park – surrounded by heaps of burning slag and holes in the ground where the surface had 'crowned in'. I would never have believed that such a landscape would one day be the site of a huge modern hospital! Now and again the ground beneath the Pensnett Railway's track would crown in and bare rails and sleepers would be suspended like a bridge until the hole was filled in again.

As well as serving the pits on the Old Park, the Pensnett Railway also continued to Scotts Green, to Weston & Wright's metalworks, and to the wharf at Wellington Road. Lines from The Wallows also ran out to pits at Himley, Pitt's brickworks, and Baggeridge Colliery, as well as out to Wall Heath and Ashwood Basin. (We had some incoming sand and gravel traffic on that line.)

In the other direction the Pensnett Railway crossed the GWR on the level and went into Round Oak Steel Works. Just before Level Street there was another coal wharf where coal was sold to dealers serving customers in Brierley Hill. Then the line passed the engine house and descended a rope-worked incline down to the Saltwells. Down in the 'coppice' was another Pensnett Railway office and a weighbridge where all the trucks from companies other than the Pensnett Railway were checked. If there were serious differences between their tare weight as stated on the wagon and their actual weight the GWR would have to be informed and they would send someone to investigate. Demurrage had to be calculated by number-takers, keeping account of wagons going in and out of customers' sidings, and accounts had to be sent to the GWR office, next door to Round Oak Station, as they kept track of their own wagons, and those of the other main-line companies. All this checking and accounting was done very precisely and very fairly so relations were good between the Pensnett Railway and the GWR. The Pensnett Railway also submitted separate accounts to other users of the railway like Weston & Wright, Constable Hart, and Baggeridge Colliery.

As the junior in the office, I was sent out on number checking duties at the pits on the Old Park. It was a very wet and dirty place. If I started out early in the summer when the mornings were light I could see the men come out of the pits at the end of the shift – very wet and covered in mud – and there were no baths at the pits for them to get cleaned up. I had to be back at the office for 9.30 a.m. when there was a break for breakfast, and if I got back earlier I could have a longer break.

The office was run by J.D. Shaw, known as Jim, who was a very nice man and excellent clerk who knew very aspect of the business. The manager of the Pensnett Railway was Frank Blackburn and beneath him was a transport manager named 'Si' Hickman (see page 114). Day to day control of traffic movements was in the hands of area inspectors. I remember the names of men like Mr Williamson, Mr Hobson, Mr Leonard Naden, Mr Mace, and there were at least two others. Three of the inspectors worked the three shifts in Round Oak Steel Works, and looked after traffic just within the works. The others worked 'days': Mr Naden down at the Coppice, Mr Mace in the Himley/Baggeridge area, and Mr Williamson in the Wallows/Old Park area. My job frequently involved finding the inspector and relaying messages that came in on the railway's own internal telephone system.

I also remember the elderly men who had worked on the Pensnett Railway for many years to become engine drivers. They had started out as young lads as cleaners and then graduated to become shunters. Eventually they had graduated to the footplate itself to become a fireman. When there was a vacancy they could become a driver. I remember Charlie Mace and William Mace, Enoch Roughton, James Wentworth, Mo Bradley, Ben Cutler, Harry Wiggin, Ted Wood and Jim Edmunds.

The drivers could work on any part of the Pensnett Railway but generally kept to their own area, which they got to know very well. Sometimes a driver was not available to work his usual patch as on that day his engine was due for a wash-out, and of course the drivers in the works had to work shifts. Being a shunter was the most dangerous part of the long process of working towards the moment when one could become a driver. The shunters had to run around coupling and uncoupling the wagons. It is a wonder that accidents were not more frequent, as there were many obstructions everywhere and shunters had to dodge point blades, holes in the ground, loose track parts, as well as keep clear of moving wagons. One shunter, Freddy Mason from Gornal, was killed, and I recall that Ben Cutler was on the footplate at the time. It was possible to hook

Peter (Andrew Barclay 0-6-0ST 1965 of 1929), photographed in 1959 with Harry Wiggin, one of the drivers known to Vernon Lovatt, on the footplate. The Pensnett Railway's locomotive *Peter* is not to be confused with the Shut End Railway's locomotive with the same name. (Viv Morgan Collection)

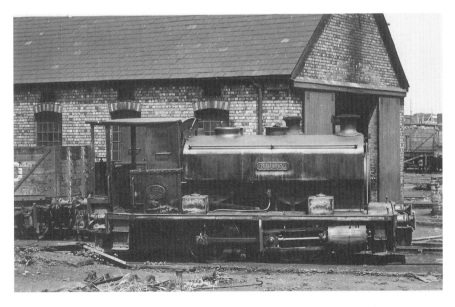

Billy (Andrew Barclay 0-4-0ST 1881 of 1925), photographed in about 1955. *Billy* was one of the locomotive names remembered by Vernon Lovatt half a century later. Many of the Pensnett Railway's engine names related to members of the Ward family, i.e. the family of the Earls of Dudley. (Roger Carpenter Collection)

the coupling pole across the end of a wagon and to ride on the pole – a practice that was expressly forbidden by the company – but shunters occasionally did it.

The chief inspector was Mr Pyatt, from Gornal, and he walked miles and miles every day checking the state of the track. And there was Harold Naden (Len Naden's brother) who was in charge of the engineering shops. I can also remember the names of the locomotives on the Pensnett Railway – some of which seemed quite odd. The oldest engines that I remember seeing being used in my time were the *Edward*, *Alexandra* and *Billy*.

The highlight of the year was the annual fete organised at Himley Park by Lord Ednam, the Earl of Dudley's son. These fetes usually ran for an entire week in August, and the Pensnett Railway was put to use to convey passengers from The Wallows up to Himley. Very temporary platforms were erected at both places and the service was very well used.

I gave up two days of my annual August holiday to volunteer to help check the tickets as people arrived at The Wallows. Every employee at the steelworks was issued with free tickets, and these had to be produced at the Pensnett Railway office before joining queues of people waiting to join the trains. The mornings would start with a trickle of people arriving from 9.30 a.m. onwards, and by the end of the morning it was extremely busy and The Wallows area was full of people with baskets of food and bottles of tea, and children everywhere. There was a very festive atmosphere and it was enjoyable to take part in it all – there was never any trouble.

At Himley Hall, Lady Rosemary (the earl's wife) and Lady Patricia (his sister) would come out of the hall with boxes of sweets for the children – which generally caused a stampede, but that didn't spoil the atmosphere. Games, sports, and refreshment facilities were laid on, and at the end of the day the children looked forward to the exciting train ride back to Round Oak, during which the engine would really work hard to propel its train up the Barrow Hill Incline. It was late in the evening by the time the trains had completed all the necessary trips.

I had occasion to travel over the Pensnett Railway at various times, but seldom travelled on the footplate as it was so dirty. Sometimes I had to take wages out to the crossing keepers who were not able to desert their posts to come and collect their wages, and sometimes I took the wages to the man who drove the stationary steam engine on the rope-worked incline. I loved going into the engine room, seeing the pistons working, and the huge drum taking in or letting out the rope. The incline seemed to be busy all day, and at the beginning and end of each day the locomotive working that part of the railway had to traverse the incline. Usually the rope provided assistance but once or twice the engine was known to make its own way up.

The men who worked on the Pensnett Railway were a grand lot – they could sometimes be 'rough and ready', but they were easy to get on with and had a

The Pensnett Railway's operation produced quite a lot of paperwork – some of which was dealt with by Vernon Lovatt as the 'office junior'. This consignment note related to just 1 ton of coal. (Alan Hallman Collection)

Vernon Lovatt's account of his work on the Pensnett Railway reminds us that drivers were among the aristocrats of the railway's staff. Vernon's own work reminds us that much of the effort used to keep the Pensnett Railway moving was concerned with quite modest and less exciting work like endlessly checking wagons – their state of repair, the weight of their load, and the time they spent in sidings. This picture was taken on 19 April 1952 and shows wagons, many with their side-doors hanging open, standing in the siding by the loop near Sandfield Bridge. (Tim Shuttleworth)

sense of humour. No one was very wellpaid, and in the early 1930s the future of the works seemed a bit precarious. At one time the Earl of Dudley gave a talk at Round Oak to say how serious things were. Some thought he was just making idle threats, but I think it was true. I think it was the skill of men like the company secretary, Mr Ballantyne, and the managing director who brought the firm round.

I stayed on the Pensnett Railway until the Second World War came along and left in 1940 to go into the army.

Pensnett Railway seven-plank coal wagons in the fuel dump at Round Oak Steel Works in about 1963. It is surprising how many wagons were used simply on an 'internal basis' in meeting the needs of the works, to which must be added wagons that left the system, and wagons that brought coal to the numerous landsale wharves. (Viv Morgan)

Les Gregory's Memories of the Himley Fete Trains

Although the trains operating in conjunction with the Himley Hall fetes from 1928 to 1937 have passed into local legend and folklore, it is quite difficult in 2013 to find anyone who can talk about them from first-hand acquaintance. I therefore include recent comments made by Les Gregory of Holly Hall:

> About 1934, my Aunt Ada took me for a ride on the Pensnett Railway while it was carrying passengers to Himley Hall for one of the Earl of Dudley's fetes. Officially tickets were only sold to employees at the Round Oak Steel Works, but Ada lived in the same street as someone who worked there and was therefore able to obtain tickets.
>
> Although I was only about 8 at the time, I was used to rail travel as about once a month I travelled by train from Dudley to Evesham to see my parents. I was therefore quite shocked by what we encountered on the Pensnett Railway. We joined the train at The Wallows by means of a very temporary platform made of planks. I was surprised to find bars on the windows (fitted as a result of the very tight fit beneath the Pensnett Railway bridges) and was also disturbed to find that we were locked in our compartment for the journey. The coach seemed quite old.

Although this photograph was found in the Keith Gale Collection, it is tempting to believe that it dates from T.R. Perkin's 1910 visit to the Pensnett Railway. Mr Perkins may even be the man in the bowler hat. It seems likely that *Countess* has been drawn up behind *Queen*, as the latter was the engine on which Perkins travelled, and he specifically identified *Countess* as the oldest engine he was shown. (Keith Gale Collection)

I remember looking out of the window as we crossed the high embankment above Fens Pool and felt frightened by the sheer drop at the side of the track. At Himley, another temporary platform was erected and it was only a short walk into the grounds of Himley Hall. I remember a band playing – I think it may have been the Woodside Band – and I have a clear memory of the Countess of Dudley tossing toffees to the children. That was my only trip on the Pensnett Railway.

T.R. Perkin's Account of the Pensnett Railway.

Thomas Richard Perkins was born in Wolverley, Worcestershire, in 1873, and grew up to become a pharmacist with a shop at 135 High Street, Henley-in-Arden. He is quite well known as a railway enthusiast because he was an early proponent of the idea that one should try and travel over every mile of railway track in the British Isles. He wrote articles on his travels and presumably took photographs. He usually travelled with a companion, who also may have taken photographs, and he usually left his wife to look after the shop while he was away. He visited the Pensnett Railway early in 1910 and published a two-part account of his trip in the May and June 1910 editions of *The Locomotive*.

In retirement, T.R. Perkins and his wife (Lily Elizabeth) came to live in Alexandra Road, Wolverhampton, a few streets away from where this book has been written. He died on 1 December 1952.

He explained to readers that his interest in the Pensnett Railway had been stimulated by seeing *Agenoria* in London's Science Museum, and goes on to say: 'We were surprised and delighted to find that the present day traffic over the celebrated line is worked by a staff of locomotives possessing an interest little inferior to that of *Agenoria* herself.'

T.R. Perkins and his companion were to some extent more interested in the locomotives of the Pensnett Railway than in the railway's workings and the geography of the system. Nevertheless, his articles do provide a first-hand account of a visit to the line in 1910 and therefore are of great interest. They began their visit at Ashwood Basin, having presumably driven there by car:

> At the foot of the incline, the locomotive *Queen*, which Mr Mantle had put at our disposal for the trip, awaited us, and before mounting the footplate, we both took the opportunity of inspecting this most interesting engine – an 0-6-0 side tank built by Manning Wardle in 1865, which is in practically original condition, with fine fluted copper dome on a square setting – it remains an excellent example of locomotive practice of the time.

They set off from Ashwood and comment on crossing the Wolverhampton–Worcester road on the level at Wall Heath, and crossing the Wolverhampton–Kingswinford road on a bridge:

> A few hundred yards beyond this bridge the present main line diverges from the original Shut End Railway by a sharp curve to the left, the remaining portion of the old line now being chiefly used as a means of access to Messrs Foster's collieries. The Shut End Incline is almost entirely unused.
>
> The semi-circular detour which the main line takes between Kingswinford and Pensnett enables it to touch several collieries in the Himley district. Two junctions, some half a mile apart, afford connection with a mineral branch of the GWR extending towards the new colliery in Baggeridge Wood. The Baggeridge extension has only been completed within the last two years.

This observation confirms the view that the lines up to Baggeridge were indeed completed well before the colliery commenced production in 1912, but, of course, they were always worked by the Pensnett Railway rather than the GWR. When they reached the foot of the Barrow Hill Incline, T.R. Perkins observed that *Queen* was moved to the back of the train to propel the wagons up the rope-hauled incline itself. This was the first indication that they had joined a working

All good things come to an end! Run-aways on the Barrow Hill Incline were a problem, hence trains were eventually always propelled up the incline. On 24 April 1935 this 'pile-up' was photographed at the foot of the incline. (Keith Gale Collection)

train as opposed to touring the system in a light engine. As the train passed under Pensnett Road, readers of the May magazine had to wait for the next month's edition to read about the rest of the journey.

The second part of the report comments on crossing the embankment by Fens Pool and remarks on some primitive signalling observed on the approach to The Wallows. At this point they left the footplate to be shown round the marshalling yards and the sheds and works, although heavy repairs at that time were still being carried out at Castle Mill Works. Mr Mantle went out of his way to allow the visitors to inspect a wide variety of Pensnett Railway locomotives. T.R. Perkins thought that five were of very Victorian appearance and noted that *Countess* of 1859 was 'the most primitive locomotive still in use'. He listed five locomotives which he saw that had been rebuilt at the Castle Mill Works (*Victory*, *Edward II*, *Alexandra*, *Dudley* and *Alma*) and was told that *Round Oak* was currently in the works. He 'spotted' four 'modern' locomotives before resuming his tour.

Back on the footplate it seems he was offered a trip up to the Dudley Branch but dismissed that as being of little interest. He probably enjoyed the excitement of the Pensnett Railway's level crossing with the GWR and the entry into the steelworks. It seems likely that he descended the Tipsyford Incline and toured the Saltwells lines, but the trip round The Wallows and the sight of all the locomotives had been the climax of his trip. At least forty years later, Keith Gale and T.M. Hoskison had the sense to travel to the Dudley Branch and even took some photographs.

Sources

Keith Gale and Thomas Michael Hoskison produced two books called *The History of the Pensnett Railway*, one published by The Cottage Press (John Horsley Denton) in 1969, based on a manuscript completed in 1951, and the second by Goose & Son in 1975 based on an update produced by Keith Gale. Michael Hoskison undertook a great deal of primary research into the papers of the Earl of Dudley's estate before they were lost, destroyed or in some cases passed to Dudley Library. He and Keith also had the advantage of knowing Frank Blackburn (one-time Pensnett Railway manager) and countless other people associated with the railway. A great source of information to everyone was *The Acorn* – a staff magazine started at Round Oak Steel Works at Christmas 1955. George Chatham took over as editor in 1959 and played a key part in making sure memories and images of the Pensnett Railway were preserved for posterity. His own booklet, *Steam at Round Oak*, was a milestone publication in its time. George Chatham used the work of photographers like Douglas Heath, and I thank the Heath family for their contribution.

Dudley Archives and Local History Service has a collection of material relating to the Pensnett Railway and I thank them for allowing me to inspect it, and to reproduce certain photographs. The archive's collection of 1880s maps is extremely useful. A small number of photographs can also be seen in the Kidderminster Railway Museum on the Severn Valley Railway. The Alan Godfrey Maps – modern reproductions of 'turn of the century' large-scale maps – are a wonderful resource and often contain useful notes – e.g. Angus Dunphy supplies information on the Himley Coalfield with the Gornal map.

About the Author

Ned Williams came to the Black Country as an 18-year-old student in 1962, and it was love at first sight as he made his first bus journey across the Black Country from Old Hill to Dudley, via Netherton. As a life-long railway enthusiast, it took him some time to understand the complexities of the local railway system, but he stumbled upon the Earl of Dudley's Railway early on while exploring the region by motorbike and on foot. Despite a desire to write world-shaking novels or prize-winning screenplays, Ned eventually settled on writing about local history, enthused by the formation of the Black Country Society in 1967, which Ned quickly joined. As a 'furriner', he has always been interested in every part of the region, although he has learnt that for most Black Country folk the word local, as in the phrase 'local history', means *intensely* local. He has had to take this on board when writing about Dudley, his first home in the area, and then Wolverhampton, his second home. The essence of what is local has become even more apparent, as Ned ventured into Quarry Bank, Brierley Hill and Netherton.

When looking back on over fifty years of living in the Black Country and writing about it, Ned's books have gone back and forth between explorations of small Black Country townships, with topic-related books that have tried to take in the region as a whole (such as books on cinemas, shops, theatres and the fairground world). In *The Earl of Dudley's Railway* (his forty-ninth book), we are back to the micro-world of looking at just one little bit of railway. Yet, however many books an author can write, or however long one lives in the Black Country, a 'furriner' is always a 'furriner'; nevertheless, Ned was allowed to become President of the Black Country Society for one year.

Keep up with Ned and his endless exploration of the Black Country by taking a look at his website: www.nedwilliams.com

If you enjoyed this book, you may also be interested in …

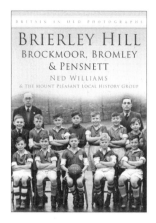

Brierley Hill: Brockmoor, Bromley & Pensnett

NED WILLIAMS & THE MOUNT PLEASANT LOCAL HISTORY GROUP

This book sets out on a journey across Brierley Hill that begins at the parish church and ends at one of the principal crossroads in the town centre, and then we make our way around the satellite communities of Brockmoor, Bromley and Pensnett. We find ourselves in a world that was dominated by many local pits where coal and fireclay were extracted, much of this coal being used in the manufacture of iron. When steel came along, Brierley Hill became the home to a large and important steelworks at Round Oak. With over 200 historic and fascinating photographs, this book is a must-have for locals and visitors alike.

978 0 7524 5563 1

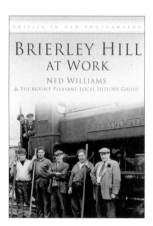

Brierley Hill At Work

NED WILLIAMS & THE MOUNT PLEASANT LOCAL HISTORY GROUP

Brierley Hill was one of those Black Country towns which was identified by the work that went on within its boundaries. Everyone knows that Brierley Hill made steel and sausages and fine pieces of glassware. These activities are now in the past but the memory of such work lingers on while the town wrestles with the problems of regeneration. This book pays plenty of attention to steel, pork products and glass, but also provides a glimpse of the many other aspects of work that have made Brierley Hill such a busy place.

978 0 7524 6511 1

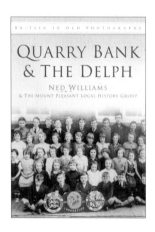

Quarry Bank & The Delph

NED WILLIAMS & THE MOUNT PLEASANT LOCAL HISTORY GROUP

This is Ned Williams and the Mount Pleasant Local History Group's third book about Quarry Bank and this time they take a fresh look at this little Black Country township, plus the even smaller place next door – simply known as The Delph. The area covered is part of the modern Metropolitan Borough of Dudley – the capital of the Black Country. All human life was to be found in these communities of colliers, brickyard workers and bucket-bashers before the days when motorists roared by on their way to the Merry Hill shopping centre. This collection of old photographs will make you pause awhile and explore some of the old shops, chapels, canals, vanished industrial enterprises, workshops and byways you never knew existed.

978 0 7524 5134 3

Visit our website and discover thousands of other History Press books.

www.thehistorypress.co.uk